tional markets (in the early 1930s). He was one of the first to invest substantially in the conquest of space (through General's subsidiary Aerojet-General).

Bill O'Neil was one of the first executives to maintain aircraft for business use. His penchant for finding successful new approaches to replace old techniques ranged from the invention of tire-display racks and development of the industry's first oversize tire to the utilization of intensive and imaginative radio, TV, and billboard advertising.

A Whale of A Territory is an engrossing portrait of a volatile, unpredictable, impulsive industrial genius. Bill O'Neil had a passion for conversation, quick humor, and great warmth for family and employees. He founded the last major company that has survived in the tire-manufacturing industry. He had great faith that "General Tire know-how" would work in any industry faced to the future—and proved it by piloting General into a billion-dollar corporate complex that operates in the fields of rubber, chemicals, plastics, airlines, missiles, and entertainment.

DENNIS JOHN O'NEILL (not a member of the one-*l* Akron clan), news editor and columnist, worked with Bill O'Neil for more than twenty years as creative head of D'Arcy Advertising...

A Whale of a Territory

THE STORY OF BILL O'NEIL

by Dennis J. O'Neill

McGRAW-HILL BOOK COMPANY

New York / Toronto / London

A WHALE OF A TERRITORY
The Story of Bill O'Neil

CONTENTS

A Whale of a Territory

I

W. O'Neil (signature)

WILLIAM FRANCIS O'NEIL was the way the name read on his 1907 diploma from Holy Cross College. It would not appear often that way again. Very early in his career his signature became simply _W. O'Neil._

"I sign it that way because it's more efficient. It saves time—and ink," he liked to say in later years. It wasn't true, but this was typical of him: he liked to pretend he had a business reason—a profit motive—for everything he did.

In a similar vein, he had a reason to explain why his family used only one _l_ in O'Neil. "My father had a department store in Akron," he would tell people, "and using only one _l_ saved on electric current for the sign on the store."

Always the profit motive—and always the whimsical twist of humor—memorable because the efficiency and parsimony it suggested were so alien to his real nature.

For all his success in reducing his written name to its smallest common denominator, William Francis O'Neil was never able to achieve uniformity in his name as used by his friends and associates. They were divided into three distinct groups. His wife Grace and most of his oldest and closest friends, including schoolmates, called him Will. His later contemporaries mostly called him Bill. And the majority of his associates in General Tire called him W.O.

As a result, any meeting in his office with more than a half-dozen or so General Tire people usually found him addressed by all three names. And there were nuances of relationship, depending upon the name used. W.O. never seemed to notice. Certainly he never commented on it.

Mindful of the O'Neil Irish ancestry, one associate had this to say of the triune names: "St. Patrick used the shamrock to explain the Trinity; here at General Tire we have Will, Bill, and W.O., three aspects of one boss."

Bill O'Neil had a passion for informality that expressed itself in many ways. For instance, there was his faithful patronage of the company cafeteria. Not in an executive dining room—he did not believe in them and would not have one—but in the crowded, noisy company cafeteria open to all W.O. would patiently await his turn to pick up his tray, keeping up a conversation with whoever was near him in line.

He was strictly a meat-and-potatoes man. No vegetables. No salad. He loved chicken; once, as a young man in the tire business in Kansas City, he won a bet from two young motor-row friends by eating nothing but chicken six days a week (Fridays, of course, excluded) for a month. When he and his wife began to go to Miami Beach and vacation at the original Flamingo Hotel, W.O. enjoyed eating lunch every day at the busiest drugstore soda fountains he could find in the neighborhood. A favorite was Fox's Drug Store, at Lincoln and Alton roads. There he could get a hot roast beef sandwich, plenty of conversation, and a thick chocolate milkshake—a perfect lunch. He would much rather have lunch there than at the exclusive Bath Club, of which he was a member, and where in those days they had an orchestra and dancing during the lunch hour. W.O. liked desserts, especially cake with chocolate frosting, or apple pie. The General Tire cafeteria always had good food of this type—and "too many kinds of vegetables and salads," W.O. thought. Chicken was not on the menu often, but there was a "Turkey Special" every year before Thanksgiving and Christmas. W.O.'s eyes always lighted up when he saw it; it never failed to come as a pleasant surprise and made the holidays more festive.

After paying the cashier, W.O. would pick up his tray and carry it to the first vacant chair at any of the cafeteria's long tables, seating eight or twelve persons. He preferred the company of people with a sense of humor but seemed to trust entirely to luck. He had no reserved table and no regular table companions. He might bring along someone who happened to be in his office at lunchtime. A visiting dealer or long-retired General Tire employee back on a sentimental visit. A job applicant. A Jesuit on his way from Holy Cross to a mission in the Far East. A newspaper reporter. An official of a foreign government, representing a country in which General Tire had a plant or was being induced to build one. The categories were endless. Sometimes there were small disparate groups that W.O. just happened to run into on the elevator. Or he might attach himself to a group of General Tire executives or stenographers on his way, and eat with them. All W.O. needed to be happy was someone to talk to.

Everyone recognized this as a normal, genuine way of life with Bill O'Neil. It was taken for granted and no one ever commented on it. Not even the most cynical ever believed it was in any sense a pose, designed to enhance his image with the workers. He argued with them too freely for that. He ate there because it was General Tire's place to eat, so it was the best place in town. Also, it was quick. And you might get a little work done talking to people while you ate.

Bill O'Neil believed that the home-made apple pie which the cafeteria served on Friday was particularly good and usually tried to sell it to everyone at the table. One day, a young man not long with the company happened to be at W.O.'s table and did not have a piece of the pie. W.O. tried to sell him the idea of having one, but the young man politely refused. "No thanks, Mr. O'Neil, I'm on a diet." "Have a piece of pie and work it off," W.O. retorted.

In later years, after a freeway was built from downtown Akron past the General offices, it was possible to get to one of Akron's several better restaurants in a very few minutes. Some of the executives and other office people started the habit of going out to lunch. W.O. didn't say much about it, but he didn't like it. Actually, his feelings were hurt. He couldn't understand how any General Tire man could prefer to eat in an outside restaurant.

Bill O'Neil was a devoted family man, but business was his avocation. Despite an occasional evening of bridge at home with Mrs. O'Neil and friends, especially if at least one of them was a General Tire dealer in Akron for a visit to the factory, he enjoyed nothing so much as being at his office from early morning to early evening. He had no other hobby except bridge. And the usual bridge game would be peppered by Will's talk of tires and business. The successful Indianapolis dealer William J. Coughlin remembered some of these bridge evenings as far back as the 1920s. He and W.O. were always partners; their opponents were usually Mrs. O'Neil and S. S. Poor, the sales manager and a longtime director of General Tire. Mrs. O'Neil and Sam Poor were excellent bridge players.

"W.O. played bad hands well," Bill Coughlin once recalled, "but he consistently overbid both good and bad hands. He played bridge like he conducted business, optimistically and with great style."

Bill Coughlin remembered that after the bridge game broke up, Will would insist on driving him to wherever he was staying, either the Portage Country Club or what was then the Mayflower Hotel. But seldom would W.O. drive directly to either place. If it were midnight or not too long after, W.O. would streak like a homing pigeon to the General Tire plant. "The men at the gate would let us in, of course, and never seemed surprised to see W.O. arrive in the middle of the night," Coughlin recalled. "In those days W.O. had keys to every door in the plant. Before the visit ended, he would usually use most of them. He always had some excuse to walk me all through the factory to show me something new. It was on one of these midnight excursions that I first saw the new method which Herman Kraft was developing to repair and recap truck tires. It was to make all us General Tire dealers a great deal of money from a service no one else had."

Herman Kraft was a great favorite with Bill O'Neil and, as a mark of respect and affection for Herman, W.O. named General's recapping method the Kraft System. When World War II began, this service, backed by many years of factory experience, was of great help to General Tire dealers and truck owners during the critical rubber shortage. With new-tire sales strictly rationed, many dealers literally were kept in business by their recapping services. William Jeffers, head of the Rubber Board of the United States War Production Board, frequently called on General Tire dealers in the large markets to make require-

[5]

ment surveys and recommendations. This wartime era gave General Tire dealers prestige in their markets, particularly among truck owners, and generated a sense of appreciation which enabled most of them to emerge from the wartime years with greatly enhanced sales opportunities.

Herman Kraft was a great innovator and was responsible for several General Tire firsts. But he once confessed that W.O. had a habit which made him nervous. "Every noon when he sees me in the cafeteria, he says, 'Well, Herman, what did you invent this morning?'"

Bill O'Neil was human enough and shrewd enough to recognize the correlation that sometimes exists between the creative person and the offbeat person. Once in a while he would say of someone, "He's nuts." It wasn't always possible to tell immediately whether he was complimenting a person for being original or writing him off as a crackpot. There was, however, one test as positive as litmus paper. If W.O. bothered to repeat the essential parts of the conversation with the man, and it concerned any kind of a new idea, it was a sure sign that W.O. regarded it as original and therefore worth some thought.

But from this point on it was never easy to follow W.O.'s thought processes. They might be going in any one of at least three directions. He might simply think it was a good idea. This was relatively easy to deduce. More often the idea would have suggested a different one, or possibly one completely opposite to the original suggestion. His thought processes were intricate and devious indeed, and yet he was the most direct, approachable, and affable of men. One couldn't ask for a more enjoyable seat companion on a flight around the world.

Bill O'Neil's disregard for time, and his willingness to talk to anyone about any subject, became legendary. A great many of these conversations took place in his office, with W.O. seated at his desk, if the subject were a calm one, or striding up and down if the topic agitated him—as so many did. With any slight letup in the traffic to his office, W.O. seemed to get lonesome. Several times a day he would saunter in the halls, stroll through the offices, out into the plant and the plant yard, stopping frequently to hold a conversation. This habit of walking through the offices and plant, constantly interrupting his progress with conversations—some of which led, no doubt, to fairly important on-the-spot decisions—prompted one associate to remark that "the only place around here that W.O. hasn't made a big decision at one time or another is the ladies' room."

One of the reasons his associates—and competitors—were frequently taken off guard by Bill O'Neil's ideas was his habit of starting with an idea and using it as a launching pad for a vaguely related but quite different one. A good illustration of this was what happened as a result of his first exposure to radio.

In the early 1930s, national radio shows had become the glamour advertising medium. The big stars were coming into American homes and making friends in a way never before possible. These people could influence potential customers, and W.O. had great faith in the power of the spoken word to sell ideas and products. W.O. felt that in many cases the stars received more advertising than some of the products they were paid to advertise, but this was because their sales talks were not properly prepared. One young fellow seemed to have an especially nice, easy way of weaving the advertising messages into the format of his show. So Bill O'Neil phoned his advertising agency and asked how much it would cost to sponsor Jack Benny. Characteristically, he did not ask for any listener ratings or for any other program suggestions. He had made up his mind that he wanted Benny.

The price floored him. General advertised heavily in the expensive media of national magazine and newspaper advertising, but W.O. figured that they had large equipment and inventory expenses, tons of paper to buy, and costly distribution and postal charges. Theirs was a manufacturing business and these costs he could understand. Radio, he figured, had none of these expenses, or practically none.

For days W.O. reasoned his case with everyone remotely connected with the problem. He stormed, pacing up and down his office, hands jammed into his pockets. He burned the long-distance wire to New York. In short, he reacted as he always did when his own ideas collided with an entrenched *status quo.*

Finally the temptation of being able to speak with millions of consumers in their homes became overpowering. So W.O. instructed his advertising agency to sign a contract for the Jack Benny program, including Jack's wife, Mary Livingston, tenor Frank Parker, announcer Don Wilson, and the orchestra.

The association was a success and W.O. enjoyed it immensely. During the initial weeks he found excuses to be in New York and attend the broadcasts. One reason he gave for wanting to be there was to familiarize Benny with tires—General Tires—so he could ad lib some sales points: it was Benny's knack of selling other products informally and effectively that had attracted W.O. to him in the first place. But the hazards of the technique showed up on one of the early programs. Frank Parker had just finished a popular song and Benny returned to the air to exclaim enthusiastically, "Wonderful, Frank! Wonderful! That was as smooth as General Tires!" With this remark Bill O'Neil's enthusiasm for the ad-lib commercial waned.

On the first program, Jack Benny told a story about his new sponsor and referred to him as Mr. O'Neil. On the second show he told another story and again referred to Mr. O'Neil. After that program, W.O. got his advertising man to one side and said: "I don't feel comfortable having Jack call me Mr. O'Neil. Don't make a big issue of it, but see if he'd mind calling me Bill O'Neil. It sounds more natural."

The significance of W.O.'s early association with the Jack Benny show was that it gave him his first contact with radio. No one at the time attached much importance to the interest he showed in every detail of the business. After each of the early Friday-evening broadcasts he gathered together a group from the studio, usually the producers, engineers, time salesmen, agency men—the people who were knowledgeable about radio as a business. More often than not, they would go out to a restaurant for a late supper and talk radio for hours. The studio people had never met a sponsor quite like him. He did not want to tell them how to handle his show, or talk about his business at all. He wanted to talk about theirs. A most peculiar sponsor! They liked him, not only as a big, attractive human being with wit, great personal magnetism and a naturalness that was refreshing, but also because he was obviously interested in their business and shoptalk.

Usually at the restaurant sessions, he would sell one or another a set of General Tires. He seldom missed an opportunity to do that. There was always a new face or two at these get-togethers, any one of whom might be the next eager caller at the New York General Tire store the Monday morning after hearing W.O. quietly paint a word picture of the difference between Generals and other tires. "Bill O'Neil said you'd give me a good trade-in and a good price on a set of Generals," became a familiar opening gambit of these radio friends calling at the store.

This was the seed of General Tire's eventual role as a major factor in radio and television through RKO General, today the largest independent operation in the field. W.O. learned enough about radio to know that the business was attractive to him. He felt at home in it. He felt radio to be the wave of the future. It would be a challenge—his ideas against larger entrenched forces. There is no question that he decided then that someday he would like to test them. And test them he did, very successfully.

Before leading his company into radio, Bill O'Neil was regarded by his competitors in Akron as having a singularly one-track mind insofar as tire manufacturing was concerned. In spite of all his enterprise, nonconformity, and occasionally revolutionary ideas about better tires and how to sell them, W.O. seemed interested only in selling his "cost more—worth more" Generals to those who could afford to pay the higher price for them. His only diversification was a modest and highly conventional purchase of a tire-fabric mill at Barnesville, Georgia, and a factory at Wabash, Indiana, to produce rubber mechanical goods.

During this deceptively quiet era—beginning in the early 1930s—most people either overlooked or discounted the power of his creative approach to international markets. Under a unique plan which assured the support of the peoples of more than a score of countries and cost General Tire and its stockholders a small fraction of a conventional assault on foreign markets, the General Tire flag was solidly planted around the globe. The move into these international markets was made years before conservative businesses found it profitable to expand overseas. In tires especially, huge British and European combines enjoy monopolies and low labor rates. And political instability was thought to make investments risky in many countries. For originality and long-term shrewdness this was one of the best examples of W.O.'s business genius and penchant for finding successful new approaches to replace old techniques.

As for General Tire's subsequent diversifications, they carried the company into what most people regard as a bewildering assortment of industries, bafflingly unrelated to each other. Bill O'Neil did not find them so. He made the decision to take on each one. He knew, for one thing, that all of them had common problems of management, research, production, and sales. He had great faith in what he loved to call "General Tire know-how." He believed this know-how could be applied profitably to any industry faced to the future—one based on a sound new idea, a new material (such as chemicals and plastics), and new end products fashioned from these new ideas and materials.

He was one of those rare businessmen who did not look forward to the future; he felt pursued by it. A compulsively competitive man with supreme confidence in the American system of private enterprise, he felt it was an obligation of business to keep constantly improving its methods, its materials, and its products.

He once said, "An industry is on the road to decline when the public is completely satisfied with its product. That removes the incentive for improvement and, with that gone, stagnation sets in."

It is significant that Bill O'Neil never chose to diversify merely by investing in companies that offered a safe return and taking a sideline, policy-making role—a seat on the board of directors, for instance, or a minority group of seats. He was interested only in fields—however diverse—in which his ideas could be put to work. Also, he was interested only in fields keyed to the future of America and to the needs and wants of its people. Just as he was the first to devise a workable private-enterprise approach to international markets, he was one of the first to invest substantially through General's subsidiary Aerojet-General in the conquest of space. He foresaw, too, the effects of a growing population. Not from a sociological point of view, though. That was not his role; the -*ologies* left him cold. But he knew that expanding populations were inevitable and would mean the eventual necessity for millions of new jobs—automation or no—and new opportunities for vastly expanded sales and services.

When Bill O'Neil organized The General Tire & Rubber Company in 1915, he visualized building a better automobile tire, one that would travel "the second 10,000 miles" instead of the 3500 uncertain miles of the tires of the time. He led the company to the development of Nygen, the tire cord which is actually stronger, pound for pound, than steel cable. He sparked the research that led to the discovery of oil-extended rubber, a basic invention which was accorded the protection of a U.S. patent in 1960. He saw General's research people initiate a chemical compound that binds tread rubber to synthetic cord so much better than other binders that it is sold to other tire manufacturers under the trade name Gentac.

There is no question that many of the scientific breakthroughs of World War II that affected the tire industry convinced Bill O'Neil that cotton and rubber—products of nature—had had their day. Man-made chemicals—synthetic rubbers, fibers, plastics, and other compounds—were the building blocks of the future. If this were true for tires, why not for many other fields? The broad dreams that lie beyond the horizons of that question are still successfully pursued at General. They have projected the company into the space age with Aerojet-General, itself a symbol of an area for exploration and enterprise in which there are no horizons, no limitations (or practically none) on imagination, enterprise, and know-how.

This is the kind of world Bill O'Neil liked and did more than his share to help create.

2

Genesis

"THE O'NEILS are a family of large families," Bill O'Neil said. "My father had seven children, and I had six until Hughie lost his life during the war. The list of all the descendants since my grandfather brought over his nine from Ireland in 1851 reads like the Book of Genesis."

"Genesis," he mused. "I like that word; it sounds like a General Tire product."

When Bill O'Neil's mother, Patience Mahar O'Neil, died in 1960 after her first illness, at the age of ninety-three, she left 33 grandchildren and 123 great-grandchildren. She had come to Akron as a bride of eighteen. Her husband, Michael, had a 20-foot one-floor dry-goods store. They arrived by horse and buggy from Patience's home in Cleveland after their marriage in St. John's Cathedral. It was an unusual double ceremony in which Patience's sister also became the bride of Thomas F. Walsh, whose family later became prominent in the Akron area. The date was July 16, 1884.

Five years later Patience encouraged her husband to go ahead with his dream of owning his own store building. Its four magnificent stories changed Akron's skyline.

Knowing Patience, one has the feeling that at twenty-three, standing on the sidewalk and looking up to the top of Michael's wonderful new building, she experienced a greater thrill from her husband's achievement than from General Tire's later successes in outer space.

Patience was interested in General's prolific diversifications. No new field of enterprise surprised her. She had seen so much of change; so much variety had come into everyone's daily life since the day of her horse-and-buggy drive from Cleveland that she knew the demands for change and variety in American life were never-ending. Just as Michael's little dry-goods store had been outmoded by the demand for a kaleidoscope of new products only a department store could offer, so other kinds of business had to furnish ever-growing kinds of new merchandise to satisfy the growing wants of people.

Patience took no part in the business affairs of the men in her family, but she had a quiet, philosophical view of business. Deeply religious, Patience once said, "Only the spiritual values never change; a business has to keep up-to-date." A casual remark of hers to Michael became the official motto of his store: *If it isn't fair to everybody, it isn't good business.*

There is no doubt that Will O'Neil derived comfort and moral courage from having his mother alive and alert almost his entire life. Patience O'Neil was known for her spirit and enthusiasm throughout her family-centered, community-conscious life in Akron.

At seventy-five, Patience took harp lessons for the first time; at eighty-five, she began traveling by plane, principally between Cleveland and her winter home in Florida. The last few years of her life her children insisted that a nurse accompany her on these trips. The year before her fatal illness, she took care of the nurse, who fell sick.

Patience reared seven children. Will was the oldest. Augustine—that was Michael's middle name—was the second son; he became a lawyer and judge in Akron. Thomas was the only son who did not graduate from Holy Cross. He attended Notre Dame and was a close friend of the late Knute Rockne until the latter's death in a plane crash in 1931. Tom was associated with General Tire during its formative years, but he never enjoyed robust health and died comparatively young, in 1943. Cyril, the youngest of the boys, became head of General's international interests and was a longtime member of the board of directors until his death July 13, 1965. There were also three daughters: Patience, who married Hugh Garvey of Sharon, Pennsylvania; Mary, who became Mrs. Henry McGinness of Shaker Heights, Ohio; Annetta had died in her early twenties.

Another important member of the family in the earlier years was Patience O'Neil's brother, Father Thomas Mahar, pastor of their parish church of St. Vincent. It was Father Mahar who introduced Patience and Michael, during a church social Patience had come from Cleveland to attend. Michael was present because he was on the parish council. Father Mahar was a dedicated pastoral priest, active among his parishioners; he aided them as children, counseled on family matters, and helped them find jobs. Many went to work at the M. O'Neil department store. Later, their children and grandchildren did the same at General Tire. Father Mahar was the first priest of the Diocese of Cleveland (in which Akron is located) to be educated and ordained at Rome. He was an educator at heart and took a great interest in his school. It was he who recommended Holy Cross College to Michael and Patience O'Neil for their sons and thus began a tradition now in its third generation. Father Mahar's tangible memorial in Akron is St. Thomas Hospital. Started with a gift of $100,000 from Michael O'Neil, the hospital was named in honor of Father Mahar's patron saint.

All four sons of Michael and Patience O'Neil were given the middle name Francis because Patience had a special devotion to St. Francis of Assisi, the patron of the poor. Will had no quarrel with the saint, but he disliked the name and, as noted, dropped even the initial from his signature. Michael also had a strong opinion about his sons' names. No son was named Michael, a result of his extreme dislike for the nickname Mike. This probably explains, too, the Spartan brevity of his adopted signature and the store name, M. O'Neil, to be followed by his son's preference in the same tradition for W. O'Neil. As things turned out in Akron later, it was better to have an M. O'Neil and a W. O'Neil anyway. Things would not have been the same for W.O., the town, or the rubber industry, if W.O., as the oldest son, had been called Junior.

Michael O'Neil was born on a farm in County Cork, Ireland, December 12, 1850, youngest of the nine children of James and Catherine Walsh O'Neil. Nearby was the Ford farm, from which Henry Ford's ancestor had earlier come to Canada before he settled in Detroit.

The James O'Neil family emigrated to New York City in the spring of 1851, when Michael was only a few months old. When he was fifteen, his father died; at the time Michael was attending LaSalle Institute. At sixteen, he went to work as a messenger boy for a Wall Street broker and lost his job on Black Friday—September 24, 1869. In the crash of the gold market and the ensuing panic young Michael lost not only his job; he also lost all interest in the stock market.

His next job was as a wholesale dry-goods clerk. He liked the business, but the dry-goods lines of the day were limited, confined mostly to staple items on which profit margins were slim and competition keen. Michael decided to look for a different product that could be sold in reasonable volume and provide a higher profit. He found it in lace.

Lace had become a very important trimming for women's dresses. The more of it that could be crowded on the better—like chrome on the automobiles of a later day, it was a status symbol, and the loftiest symbol of all was imported lace. Hadn't Michael from earliest boyhood heard his mother extol the glories of Irish lace? It was not difficult for a lad named Michael O'Neil to establish cordial contacts with lacemakers in Ireland. He became an expert, and before long the importing was the most profitable part of his business.

Later he learned about the fine French laces which came in greater varieties and were very much in vogue. In a matter of months, Michael taught himself to read and write French in order to be able to read French trade journals, to write for lace samples, and to order directly. W.O. always said his father learned the language so he could understand the prices. At any rate, Michael did subscribe to French trade journals until his death—mostly, in later years, to help him retain his knowledge of the language.

During this period, Portuguese immigrants were also establishing small colonies on Cape Cod. The womenfolk filled the long hours of waiting for their fishermen husbands by making exquisite lace. Michael acquired a speaking knowledge of Portuguese. He was able to talk to the lacemakers of these villages and was soon buying their entire output. Michael's Portuguese lace had a great commercial advantage, too. It had a stylish "imported" sound to it, but came from that bastion of Yankeeland, Cape Cod, and there was consequently no duty to pay.

Before his twenty-seventh birthday, in 1877, Michael had accumulated enough capital to open his first dry-goods store. He may have chosen Akron because it was at the junction of two busy canals. One ran from north to south, from Lake Erie to the Ohio River; the other—the Pennsylvania and Ohio or "Cross Cut" Canal—eastward to Pittsburgh. It had been incorporated as a city, with a population of 5060, just thirteen years before. Great growth was predicted for the city because of the fortunate location. Also important to the young merchant was the fact that many Irish immigrants had settled there after building the canals.

Within the next ten years the "Cross Cut" Canal to Pittsburgh was filled in, creating what is still the widest business street in Akron, Main Street. To Michael it was obvious that this broad thoroughfare in the heart of town was going to be valuable business property. No one else seemed to think so, and Michael was able to acquire a good deal of land. One parcel he visualized as the site of a future store, much larger than the twenty-foot-wide single floor he occupied at 114 East Market Street. Other parcels were acquired nearby in checkerboard fashion to prevent the building of another large store near his future one. Farsighted indeed!

Michael had taken a partner in his original store. a young Dubliner he had known in New York with the singularly un-Irish name of Isaac Dyas. The store continued on East Market Street, under the name O'Neil & Dyas, until 1889. Then, in February, O'Neil & Dyas moved into its own four-story stone building on the South Main Street site Michael had selected. Eight months later it was destroyed by fire, and the two Irish merchants were back in their twenty-foot store, making change out of their pockets.

Michael was in New York on a buying trip when the fire broke out. He was notified by telegram and returned by overnight train in time to see the ruins still smoldering. He watched them for a long time from across the wide street, and finally sat down on the curb dejectedly. He never knew how long he sat there; but watching him was Ferdinand Schumacher, Akron's first citizen of the time and known as the "Cereal King of America." A native of Hanover, Germany, Schumacher had started an oatmeal mill in Akron some years earlier. He made oatmeal as he had seen it made in Germany. Up to his time, all the oatmeal in America had been imported. His business was successful and eventually, after a series of mergers, became part of the Quaker Oats Company.

At length, Schumacher—thirty years Michael's senior—sat down beside him.

The older man was the first to speak. "Well, Michael, it's all gone. How much was it worth?"

"Three hundred thousand dollars."

"How much insurance?"

"Just $109,000 worth. The building was fireproof."

According to Michael, that was all the conversation there was. Ferdinand Schumacher drew a checkbook from the inside pocket of his five-button burgomeister jacket and, still sitting on the curb, wrote in pencil his check for $200,000 to Michael O'Neil. There was no note asked or given. The sequel to this story is that many years later, long after the loan had been repaid, Schumacher's fortunes declined and he was in a critical position in the grain market. Desperately he needed the identical sum he had loaned to Michael in his time of need. Michael furnished the money, on the same terms as their original transaction. Unfortunately, the loan did not prevent Schumacher from going bankrupt later. Legally, he was obliged to list M. O'Neil's $200,000 loan as a liability; but according to Michael's account, Mr. Schumacher paid the debt in full before his death.

The Schumacher curbstone loan enabled Michael to start rebuilding his store immediately. Exactly a year to the day of the fire—October 28, 1890—O'Neil & Dyas moved into its new building. A short time after the new store was in operation, Isaac Dyas died. Thereafter the store was known as the M. O'Neil Company.

It is quite remarkable that Michael O'Neil, highly successful in Akron, its leading merchant, largest owner of downtown buildings, community leader and philanthropist, stood almost completely aloof from the rubber industry while the city was beginning to become the Rubber Capital of the World. He continued to interest himself very successfully in local Akron activities and opportunities—chiefly merchandising and real estate. The one important exception was a major interest he acquired in a cotton mill in Worcester, Massachusetts.

This acquisition had a relationship to the burgeoning Akron rubber industry. Shortly after the turn of the century men from the rubber companies began to experiment with different fabric materials from which to build the casings for their new pneumatic tires. Frequently they dropped into the M. O'Neil Company store to look over the available stock of fabrics. They would buy a couple yards of burlap, linen, silk, or cotton and build one experimental tire.

A cotton cloth known as *E* duck became the most popular, and most companies standardized on it. Within a year or two the rubber companies' purchases of this material were considerable, and Michael O'Neil's mill suppliers began to wonder how a department store in Akron, Ohio, could dispose of so much of their unglamorous duck. It did not take them long to find out, of course, and begin to sell direct to the rubber companies. Anticipating this, Michael had bought the interest in the Worcester mill because that was where young Will was in school. He could work in the office while going to Holy Cross College and still keep an eye on the operation.

This peripheral association with the rubber industry was Michael's only venture into Akron's wonderful world of rubber before The General Tire & Rubber Company was formed. A total of 358 rubber companies were to start in the business, most of them long on hope and short on money. Some of them were stock-promotion companies which built tires reluctantly. Others were legitimate. Akron and its surrounding communities became the rubber capital.

Michael's Worcester mill was successful during the years Will was in college, but in the end was disappointing. A new brokerage house in New York, Taylor, Armitage & Eagles, chose it and a similar mill in Passaic, New Jersey, for its first venture in merging companies by underwriting a new joint stock issue. This was one of Michael's few disappointing ventures. Possessing only nonvoting stock, he was unable to prevent the failure of the combined company. The experience probably did not enhance his faith in the tire business. The merger does, however, have a certain historical interest. The Taylor of Taylor, Armitage & Eagles was Myron Taylor, who went on from this cotton-mill promotion to become one of America's leading financiers and industrialists. In 1932 he succeeded J. P. Morgan, Jr., as chairman of the board of the U.S. Steel Corporation. In 1939 Taylor was appointed President Roosevelt's personal diplomatic representative to the Vatican, serving in this post until 1950.

3

It had to be Will

Kansas city was an unlikely place for W. O'Neil to set up in business after his graduation from college in 1907. It had been taken for granted that he would come home, go to work in his father's department store and, after a few years of seasoning, take over the top spot. Michael no doubt felt that his timing had been perfect. Now in his late fifties, he wanted to detach himself from the details of running the store, to be able to devote more time to new downtown real estate projects. He had two major ventures in mind, a new hotel and an office building. Particularly he was interested in the office building because—O'Neil-like—he planned to put a good dining room on the top floor so that tenants of the building would have a convenient place in which to take their customers to lunch.

There is a faint hint here of W.O.'s later fondness for eating lunch close to the job in the General Tire cafeteria. But Michael's idea developed somewhat differently. When Michael's building was built a few years later, first the top two and later three floors were devoted to the Akron City Club, still Akron's finest downtown businessman's club.

The basic idea of the dining room was adhered to and the Ohio Building is considered the first in America to have had dining facilities, primarily for its tenants, built into the top floors as part of the original planning.

Michael was sure that Will would take to the store—it had to be Will. Augustine had decided on a law career. Tom was in his teens, and Cyril was still in the St. Vincent parochial school. Will liked the store. He had worked there every summer and during the busy shopping days of every Christmas vacation. He liked to meet people. Especially he liked the challenge of selling new ideas and products. He once said later, "The only thing I didn't like about the store was that I had to wear the clothes that other people didn't buy." He also commented, years later, on a remark former President Dwight D. Eisenhower had made about his own boyhood in Abilene, Texas: "We were poor but didn't know it." Will O'Neil said, "We weren't poor but I didn't know it."

As a matter of fact, the store was an exciting place for a young man. The placid dry-goods type of operation was passé. Manufacturers of many lines of apparel, home furnishings, and appliances were beginning to learn the techniques of limited mass production. Their output called for more dynamic distribution at the local level, and the emerging department store idea was the answer. These manufacturers cooperated in the cost of large-space newspaper advertising, displays, and special promotions. Methods within the store were changing, too. Cash registers were installed; M. O'Neil's is said to have been the first department store in America to have them. And there is a story—perhaps apocryphal—that Michael occasionally circulated counterfeit money in the store to keep the sales people and cashiers alert while they were accustoming themselves to this new form of automation in the handling of cash. M. O'Neil's window displays were far in advance of their times. They were attractive, changed twice a week, and tied in directly with current sales events in the store—a marked departure from the hodgepodge, seldom changed, often fly-specked window displays of the day.

Will hadn't been at the store long when, one day, a young salesman called on him to explain a new "change-over" plan his company was introducing into the dress-pattern field. His patterns were new, superior to the competition's. To induce department stores to carry them exclusively and feature them, the company would give the store an acceptable trade-in allowance on its inventory of competitive patterns. Simultaneously with the changeover, his company would share the cost of an advertising and sales-promotion effort on the new and better patterns. It is not known whether Will O'Neil went for the deal, but he did recall the idea a few years later and his application of it to the tire business had astounding impact.

Early in the autumn of 1907, underweight and weak from his last strenuous year at college, Will was sent to Denver to regain his strength. The prospect of months of inactivity doubtless dismayed him, but there is also some evidence that he welcomed the opportunity to take a little time to think things through.

The climate in Denver and the long walks he took every day did Will a great deal of good. His appetite improved and his weight increased. He does not seem to have worried much about his health—all his letters to his mother mentioned how well he was feeling—and this state of mind undoubtedly contributed to his recovery in a relatively short time.

By sometime in the fall he had taken a job; not strenuous work, but selling, of all things, trading stamps. There was a certain amount of travel involved; it kept him outdoors most of the time, and his sample case certainly wasn't heavy. This career could not have lasted very long, because by the Christmas holidays he had another job. But while he was a trading-stamp salesman he got at least one expenses-paid trip—to Boulder, Colorado, about thirty miles north of Denver. There he made an exciting sale.

The trip to Boulder was made on the type of train which must have been responsible for the phrase *accommodation train*. It accommodated the traveling salesmen from Denver who were its chief patrons. It started out from Denver in the early morning, laid over a few hours in Boulder, then returned to Denver in the late afternoon. This enabled the salesmen to make their calls and return on the same train. On the way up W.O. met another salesman who turned out to be selling trading stamps too. He was a dapper, fast-talking city-slicker type to whom W.O. was not particularly attracted, but they talked all the way to Boulder. The stranger was an experienced trading-stamp salesman from whom W.O. probably thought he could pick up some pointers. W.O. had a lifelong habit of asking questions. But he also said, much later, "If you are going to pick people's brains, first make sure whether they have any." At any rate, W.O. and his competitor parted company in the business section of Boulder to work opposite sides of the street.

In the largest store in town, W.O. found the owner behind a counter. He was belligerently opposed to trading-stamp salesmen. "The last one through here sold me a fake deal," the store owner said. "The premium merchandise was worthless. I don't blame you," he added. "You're a big fellow. This other salesman was a little, fast-talking smart aleck."

The description fitted W.O.'s seat companion on the train. They compared notes and decided the culprit was in town. Just then they saw him crossing the street, heading for the store. As the salesman entered the door, the owner said to W.O., "Quick! If you want to see some fun, get in the back room." As the salesman approached quickly, put out his hand, and began a breezy greeting, the owner, a big man, reached under the counter, pulled out an enormous revolver, and began shooting at the salesman's feet. The salesman leaped straight up—"as high as the counter," W.O. always claimed—and somehow managed a half-twist in midair so he was headed in the right direction to take off for the door in terror as soon as he lit. The episode put the store owner in such high good humor that, after the excitement subsided, he gave W.O. a substantial contract—the best one in town—and the two parted good friends.

Later, on the train, W.O.'s dapper competitor, not much subdued by his experience, expressed the opinion that "Boulder will never be the city Denver is—its merchants aren't aggressive."

Shortly before Christmas, W.O. took a job that did not require travel from Denver but still kept him in the open air. He became an "extra jumper" on a May Company department-store delivery wagon.

Years later Will said that he didn't remember much about the vehicle but that it didn't have pneumatic tires. W.O. often expressed the notion that if pneumatic tires had been available for delivery wagons and buggies, the passing of the horse might have been delayed a few years. This is one of his less-provable theories, but it is interesting because it illustrates how basic he felt the development of pneumatic tires was to creating the automobile age.

He felt that all kinds of motive power could have been developed (and indeed they were)—the internal-combustion engine, air-cooled and water-cooled; steam, electric-power and diesel—and that any of them might have survived the competitive struggle for preference, but that all had one thing in common: the vehicle had to run on rubber tires. He also felt that the internal-combustion engine won out because more research and development were devoted to it than to the others. He believed that no company could survive in a competitive industry without a big and continuous research program.

Will O'Neil's association with The May Company during that Christmas rush is of interest because, just four years later, in 1912, his father, convinced that Will was not coming back to take over at the store, sold the M. O'Neil Company to The May Company for a million dollars and a twenty-five-year lease on the building.

This figure was finally approved after several meetings had failed to shake Michael's insistence on this price. At the final meeting in a Cleveland law office, just before The May Company officials accepted the deal, Nate Dauby, the president, injected one more demurrer. "Mr. O'Neil, a million dollars is a lot of money." "I know," said Michael. "I've already made one." This closed the discussion about the price. But there was one more detail: Michael wanted $200,000 in cash. After some discussion, Michael and two May Company men went to a bank and returned with two leather handbags, each ostentibly containing $100,000. Michael's young son Tom was with him. One of the bags was given to him to carry. Michael kept the other. Father and son walked to the interurban station on Cleveland's Public Square. They had an hour's wait and Tom's nervousness mounted by the minute. Finally, the interurban car was ready for boarding and Tom clutched his moneybag tightly to him all during the long ride to Akron. The local bank was closed when they reached the station, but a phone call from Michael arranged for someone to reopen it. In the bank and with the doors locked, young Tom felt safe at last. His bag was opened first. It contained rolled-up newspapers. Michael's bag contained all of the $200,000. In later years Tom said he thought it would never catch on as a popular sport, but it was one way to have fun with $200,000.

Michael also insisted on writing into the terms of the sale to The May Company the provision that no employee of the store would ever be dismissed except for an act of dishonesty. This continued a long tradition of his store. It is remembered in Akron to this day that no store employee of Michael O'Neil's was ever discharged. Salaries and wages were not high, but everyone knew that he or she had "social security" a generation before the term became known.

In the welter of conversation that developed over the clause about retaining employees, Michael forgot to mention his desire that the name of the store be retained. The next day he telephoned Mr. Dauby and told him. The answer was: "Mr. O'Neil, without the name, the business wouldn't be worth nearly a million dollars." Ever since, the store has operated under the M. O'Neil Company name.

Four years before this, in the spring of 1908, fate had begun to rough-hew the destiny of young Will O'Neil. He met the Denver distributor for Firestone tires. This was a casual meeting. The brief conversation seems to have sparked no lifelong friendship between the two, as did so many of Will's chance meetings with different people during his lifetime. The man was merely interested in the fact that Will came from Akron. "I was in Akron last week," the man said, "visiting the factory. I thought everyone from Akron worked for a rubber company. What do you do?" There seems to have been not much more to the conversation than words to this effect except that the man added that while in Akron he had heard that the Kansas City territory for Firestone tires was open. "It's a whale of a territory—covers the whole Southwest," he added.

All the rest of the day until late in the evening, Will thought about the idea. The point that kept recurring to him was one casual remark: "It's a whale of a territory—covers the whole Southwest." He realized then the basic difference between his and his father's business philosophy and ambitions. Michael had arrived in Akron when it had been a city about ten years. He had been outstandingly successful. As the city grew, the value of his merchandising business and real estate interests expanded with it. Michael loved Akron and felt indebted to it. Now he gave increasingly of his time to civic affairs and local philanthropies. Akron was his life. Will had happy memories of a wonderful boyhood and many good friends in Akron, but he realized suddenly that the one thing he disliked about the store was that it was a local business. Furthermore, his father had reached the limit of the market's potential. Certainly it would grow as the city continued to grow, but Will refused to cast his future in so tight a mold. He knew it now. He wanted "a whale of a territory," a great big piece of America to work in—and the whole Southwest sounded like a good beginning. He would not be interested if he were going to be just the Firestone dealer in Kansas City.

That evening Will sat alone in his room and wrote a brief note to Firestone. He wanted to know only three things: whether the territory was available, how big it was, and what capital was required. He mailed the letter the same night. It had occurred to him to write first to his parents, specifically to his mother, since he knew he would have to overcome her doubts about his health. He decided, however, that after all the territory might not be open, or for any one of a dozen reasons the matter might go no further and, in that case, he would not have to take up the matter at home.

He underestimated the excitement his inquiry was to cause at Firestone. Prospective dealers with good credit ratings were rare in those days. Here was an inquiry from a son of the man with the best credit rating in Akron. Firestone's first move was to get in touch with Michael O'Neil, to learn principally whether the father would guarantee young Will's credit. Michael was incredulous. In keeping with his nature he said little, but as soon as he could hurry home to Patience—this was no news to trust to a 1908 telephone—Will's secret from his mother was out. The decision of both parents was negative. They regarded it as "an impulsive act of youth," "a harum-scarum project."

Meanwhile, Will had second thoughts about not having written to his mother. In his letter he explained that the doctor had said that he had fully regained his health and that it would be a good idea for him to go to work again. Not in an office or "in the store," but in some type of work that would keep him out in the open air a good deal. He also mentioned that he had heard about the Firestone distributorship in Kansas City and felt that it would be ideal because he would have to be out covering the territory quite a bit of the time, not confined to an office.

Will's letter was persuasive. It helped somewhat to relieve his parents' minds but by no means convinced them that their son was being sensible. Michael pondered the matter for a day or two. Then he asked Patience to write Will a letter, asking him to come home to discuss his plan. Patience suggested a telegram, but Michael vetoed this. "There is no necessity for impulsive haste," he said. "That's

Will's trouble. He's being impulsive and hasty." So the letter from Patience was posted to Will that day.

When he reached Akron, Will had less trouble than he had anticipated. His mother was not enthusiastic. But, what was important to her, her son looked better. He had gained weight; his bubbling enthusiasm was back as he talked about the Kansas City future. Finally she agreed that the experience might be good for him. Michael was more difficult to convince. He had talked to the Firestone people several times before Will had reached home and made it clear to them that he opposed the proposition. Will was only twenty-three; Michael felt that the responsibility was too great for so young a man and in turn Firestone would be put in an unfair position. Michael refused to put his credit on the line for Will's "impulsiveness."

Someone finally made a suggestion that was more businesslike in Michael's eyes although still not dazzlingly attractive. The idea was this: Will was a great salesman; granted he was not an experienced credit man. Firestone's credit manager since 1905, Winfred E. Fouse, would be a perfect partner.

Eventually Michael capitulated. Will had $3500 coming to him from Michael as his share of the profits while Will was working in the store, and Michael made this available to Will to start in Kansas City. It is believed to have been the same amount of money Michael put into his first dry-goods store in Akron. Michael also agreed to guarantee the young partners' credit up to a fixed maximum, but he was never required to exercise this obligation.

4

"The first thing
a shoe salesman does"

I T WOULD BE difficult to find two lifelong business partners of more dissimilar temperament than Bill
O'Neil and Win Fouse. Yet their very dissimilarities were
an advantage because the two men complemented one
another perfectly. W.O., the volatile, restless, imaginative
optimist—his ambitions always a long step ahead of the
immediately possible—was balanced by the calm, reasonable Fouse, the methodical inside administrator and credit
man. Their association, begun in 1908 when Will was
twenty-three and Win thirty-one, continued until Fouse's
death on July 22, 1958, just a few months short of fifty
years.

Fouse was, like Bill, a native of the Akron area. His
great-great-grandfather came to this country from Bavaria
just eight years after the signing of the Declaration of
Independence. His parents migrated from Pennsylvania
and settled at Hartville, near Akron, shortly before Win
was born. He attended public grade and high schools in
Hartville and, upon graduation, was offered a teaching

position by the local authorities because of his outstanding scholastic record. Win accepted the offer and taught for two years, saving his money to pay for a year's tuition, board, and room at Eastman Business College in Poughkeepsie, New York.

Win's first nonteaching job was with a brokerage house in Cleveland. There he became interested in the rubber activity astir in and around Akron. He decided that his acre of diamonds might lie after all in his own backyard, so he applied to the Diamond Rubber Company for a position in its accounting department. This was the beginning of Win's association with the rubber industry. The year was 1902. He remained with Diamond for three years, then in 1905 became credit manager at Firestone.

Will O'Neil and Win Fouse went to Kansas City late in 1908. In January 1909 as equal partners they formally organized the Western Rubber & Supply Company, later renamed the Western Tire & Rubber Company.

They opened their first tire store at 1737 Grand Avenue, in the heart of Kansas City's "automobile row." This was an exciting place for two young men to be in business. For that matter, any automobile row was glamorous anywhere in America. Every city of any size had one, the Disneyland of the day. People flocked about until late in the evening for the fun and excitement of seeing the shiny new cars in the brightly lighted showrooms. There were gas cars with from one to eight cylinders. Next to them steam cars, with rumors of fabulous cash awards offered by their manufacturers to anyone who would drive them "full throttle" for three minutes. There were electrics, steered by tillers, with glass bud vases as standard equipment.

The atmosphere, with its quick tempo, its combination of camaraderie and keen competitiveness, was made to order for Will O'Neil. Quickly he became well known and liked by all the dealers on the row. In a short time he was an extremely popular member of the Kansas City Club, where he formed friendships with the city's business leaders which continued through his life. One of them, a banker, recalled in 1964 that several automobile manufacturers tried to persuade Will to give up his tire agency and take on their car franchises. "I remember one such conversation especially well because I was there," one of these bankers recalled years later. "The conversation took place at lunch in the Kansas City Club. 'Tire profits are small change, Bill, compared with the profits on car sales,' the car manufacturer said. 'We have a great car; we are going to back it with a lot of advertising and we have great things planned for developing sales in this area.' This was the gist of his argument, and I'll admit he had me pretty well convinced. I thought there was more money to be made in new cars than in tires, too. A big new market was opening up; there were no used-car problems yet, or any other complications that came along later. Yes, I thought an ambitious young fellow with Bill's personality and sales ability could do a lot better with a high-profit-margin item like an automobile than with tires. But all through the conversation, Bill just gave him that lingering Irish smile of his. I don't remember what counterarguments Bill used, if any. He just wouldn't be convinced. He seemed to love the tire business."

Unquestionably one reason Bill O'Neil could not be interested in a car-dealer franchise was his determination to stay out of a local business, the one feature of his father's department store he disliked.

He was soon pressured by two forces into becoming a local businessman—by offers to become a car dealer and by Firestone's new sales plans. It became apparent after a year or so that a new factory-distribution policy caused

[35]

Firestone to regret the large territory given to Bill O'Neil and Win Fouse. All over the country, Firestone was establishing factory branches and replacing its independent agents. Will realized that sooner or later Western's territory would be reduced greatly.

Meanwhile he attacked his sprawling three-and-a-half-state domain with a vengeance. Looking back from the vantage point of more than a half-century, it is easy to dwell on the glamour and excitement of Kansas City's automobile row and emphasize the pleasant evenings at the Kansas City Club. Actually, Bill O'Neil worked his territory most of the time. Whether by automobile on short trips or by train, this was hard, day-and-night work. No wonder Bill O'Neil was one of the first major executives in the country in the late 1920s to utilize the private airplane for business trips! Road conditions were incredible and rail connections poor. It was 618 miles to Amarillo, which was in his territory; even Oklahoma City was 360 miles away. It was rough going all the way and there was no real pot of gold at the end of any of these grueling trips. Just a challenge, a chance to talk tires; try to get dealers to adopt progressive selling ideas; listen to their complaints and sell them more tires.

Most of the dealers were hardware merchants. This was true in all sections of the country, but particularly in the Southwest. Win Fouse liked them as dealers because hardware men, even in the smallest towns, usually had some kind of credit rating. Furthermore, as a rule of thumb, hardware stores had the lowest bankruptcy rate of any kind of retail business. Win told W.O. this one day and added, "Restaurants fail the oftenest. I don't know why." W.O. replied, "If you'd come out in the territory once in a while and eat with me you'd know why."

W.O.'s hardware dealers convinced him of something

he believed all the years he was in the tire business. A tire dealer should sell tires and service—nothing else. As merchandising trends changed, particularly after World War II, and tire stores added everything from radios and television sets to bicycles, toys, and phonograph records, Bill O'Neil called them *hardware stores* and took a dim view of them.

He remembered the hardware stores, piled to the ceiling with barbed wire, pipes, oil stoves, washing machines, garden tools, and hundreds of other lines which left the dealer little time to devote to tires. The tires, in fact, were usually not displayed at all. Either they were in the back room haphazardly strewn around on the floor or on a rack near the ceiling, over the coils of barbed-wire fencing.

The lack of tire display caused W.O. in 1909 to invent and have built a metal stand for displaying one tire in an upright position—a simple idea, but no one had thought of it before. Ever since, these display stands have been used universally by tire companies. Probably millions have been made and furnished to dealers; W.O. should have patented the idea. His first stands proved too light to withstand the Missouri and Oklahoma winds when used outside. So W.O. had the bottoms weighted. The dealers were supposed to put them in front of the store each morning and bring them in at closing time. Since the stores were on Main Street, the tires were safe during the daytime. Occasionally someone would forget to bring them in and a tire would disappear during the night. This prompted W.O. to add a length of chain and padlock as extra equipment so that the tire could be chained to a convenient grating or post. This feature, too, has been widely adopted and never much improved upon.

The inside diameters of tires then were much larger than they are today. Bill O'Neil, seeing one of his tires in one of his stands on a sidewalk in Sedalia, Missouri, decided one day that it should have an advertising message printed on a circular piece of cardboard to fill the large hole in the center. This was the first display "tire center," an idea also copied widely in the industry.

Because most of the hardware stores were built along Main Street sidewalk frontage, there was no service court area unless by luck there happened to be space in back with access through an alley off a side street. W.O. preached the importance of service areas. He also urged the employment of a man trained in tire care who would devote all or most of his time to tire sales and service. He told one of his hardware dealers, in Muskogee, Oklahoma: "My father had a department store in Akron, Ohio, and I used to work in the shoe department in the summertime when I was going to college. You know the first thing a shoe salesman does? He takes off the customer's shoe. Then the buyer can't walk out of the store. You should have a service yard. The first thing your man should do is to take off the customer's tire to inspect it. Then he can't drive off."

Many years later this man became a General Tire dealer. He reminded W.O. of the shoe-clerk story. W.O. used it often after that at dealer sales conferences. He thought that if the man from Oklahoma had remembered it all those years, it must be a pretty good sales story.

Some of the nonhardware dealers W.O. brought into his company worried Win Fouse, the credit man. W.O. always checked local references for a new account, usually with the town banker. "Fouse always thought the banker was the man's brother-in-law," W.O. said later. "I never blamed him for being cautious. Some of the banks out there didn't have credit ratings."

Will O'Neil's ideas about tires went far beyond originating better tire displays and promoting sales effort. He soon evolved a philosophy about tires which became the basis of his success in the tire business and had profound effect on the design evolution of all modern automobile tires. It was natural for Will to think in terms of the basic nature of the product he was selling because, as a salesman, he always believed in "selling the difference." In his father's department store he had learned that the way to sell a higher-priced product, with a lower-priced one of the same kind alongside on the counter, was to sell the advantages of the difference. Will thought this should be true of tires. But in the tires of that day there were no real differences. The prices were within pennies of each other; the mileage guarantees were about the same, usually 3500 miles, and there were no design differences of any importance.

Will thought it illogical that the basic qualities of rubber (the very ones which made rubber the only substance out of which automobile tires could be made) were not being taken full advantage of. Rubber's flexibility, its resilience, its ability to provide good traction and resist skidding made rubber ideal for automobile tires. But the tires of the day put the least amount of it possible in contact with the road. Tires were made not only with the smallest possible cross section; they also were inflated rock-hard. Will O'Neil thought this made an "iron tire" from rubber, cotton fabric, and air, three of the softest and most pliant things in nature. He felt there was no reason for this, except that a softer riding, better-skid-resistant tire, with a larger cross section, able to run at lower pressure, would naturally cost more to manufacture.

And it would require a better-educated dealer, one able to make enough profit from the sale and service of such a tire to devote full time to it. He would have to be trained in the product advantages so that he could sell the price difference.

"The least of the difference would be the difference in price," Will told Win over and over again when the two remained in their Grand Avenue office long after closing hours talking tires.

They had these after-hours talks often if Will was not out in the territory, and they continued far into the evening. They discussed routine current problems, such as what they would do if too much territory were taken away. But Will looked a great deal into the longer future. He was becoming more and more convinced that a market existed for a better tire that would cost more money. It had to cost more because it would cost more to build, and the kind of full-time, dedicated dealers he visualized as selling it would have to make a larger profit to justify the investment and effort.

Will did not consider price a disadvantage. "People naturally believe that a higher-priced product is worth more than a cheap one," he told Win. "I can remember in the department store, if you put three racks of men's ties on a counter, priced at one dollar, three dollars, and five dollars, most people, if they have the money, will buy the five dollar tie every time. Of course, a higher-priced tire would have to deliver more—more safety, a more comfortable ride, and some more mileage. It would have to be a better-looking tire. It would have to be recognized as a prestige tire instantly by its sidewall and tread. And it would have to be advertised in a prestige way. People buy an automobile because it does something for their pride of ownership. Why shouldn't they add the final touch to that feeling by equipping their car with tires that are designed to be better in performance, better-looking, and that add to their pride of ownership?" Will argued in this vein for hours. But in 1911 these were rhetorical matters for two young tire jobbers whose immediate worry was which counties Firestone would take from their sales territories next, and how soon. Getting into the tire-manufacturing business was out of the question.

Will had his eye fixed on a very important date, September 14. The preceding summer he had met a girl who would have more influence on his life than any other person. She was Grace Savage, one of the eight children of John Savage, a Kansas City contractor. Grace was a beautiful girl with auburn hair and hazel eyes. She had a lovely smile and a soft well-modulated voice. Fittingly, their romance had begun on automobile row. George Tebeau, president of the Kansas City baseball club, then in the American Association, operated an agency for the Stearns automobile across the street from Western's place of business. Will had met Tebeau through Grace's brother John, who was executive secretary of the baseball club. That summer, Grace had just begun a summertime job in Tebeau's car agency office when Will O'Neil dropped in. Fritz Oberheu, then division manager of the B. F. Goodrich Company, happened to be there. Will said later that from his office across the street he had seen Fritz go in and followed him to make sure he did not get ahead of him on any possible tire business that might result from the call. At any rate, it's a good thing that Will came in. Fritz knew Grace and introduced Will.

From that moment Will's trips across Grand Avenue became more frequent during the day, and his room at the Knights of Columbus hall saw less of him in the evenings. He also became a visitor in the Savage home. The wedding took place on September 14, 1911, in St. Aloysius Church. Father Thomas Mahar—Patience's brother and pastor of St. Vincent's—who had introduced W.O.'s mother and father, traveled from Akron to officiate at the ceremony. Two sons, Bill and Tom, were born in Kansas City before the O'Neils moved to Akron in 1915.

Early in 1911 Bill O'Neil foresaw that it would be only a matter of time before Firestone reduced his territory considerably. Western had already lost a few counties here and a few more there as the factory spread its new policy of establishing branches and replacing independent agents.

The unkindest cut—and a drastic one—in Western's territory occurred while Will and Grace were on their wedding trip. The O'Neils returned immediately to Kansas City, their honeymoon reduced to six days. Will never knew whether the factory was aware that he was on his honeymoon when the move was made. But, he said, "I never got married again."

The largest territory reduction was responsible for Bill O'Neil's first experiment in diversification. He and Fouse changed the name of their company from Western Rubber & Supply Co. to Western Tire & Rubber Company. On the surface this does not seem like much of a change; in the light of all that was to come it was significant.

For the time being, however, the most ambitious project the newly named company could undertake was the manufacture of tire-repair materials—cementless patches, tire reliners, blowout boots—the last made principally of friction materials, bristling with steel studs. The company obtained patents on some of the items. They sold because they were simple to use and rugged. The uncertain quality of the tires of the time made motorists feel more relaxed on a crosstown trip if they had an assortment of Western patches stored under the front seat.

This end of Western's business prospered. Within two years a hundred employees were on the payroll in a plant on the outskirts of Kansas City and volume grossed $500,000. It was the largest business of its kind in the country.

In 1914, this manufacturing enterprise proved a good insurance policy. The Firestone Company attempted to reduce Western's territory to that of a local Kansas City dealership. Bill O'Neil broke his agency relationship with Firestone. In spite of this, Western's profits were larger that year than ever before.

One of the most colorful tire deals of Will O'Neil's more than fifty years in the business was made in 1914. A carload of McGraw tires, then made in East Palestine, Ohio, was offered to him for $700. Apparently Will thought this price was so low he could not afford to turn it down. The McGraw was a competitive tire, with the standard 3500-mile guarantee of the day. Will was certain he could wholesale the lot to dealers and turn a quick profit, but for some reason no one wanted his bargain tires.

Eventually a hardware-store owner in southern Missouri offered to exchange the tires for twenty acres of Florida land located "twenty miles south of Ft. Lauderdale." There was no mention of Miami in the description. In desperation Will accepted the deal. Years later, the property was absorbed within the city limits of Miami. During the first Florida land boom of the early 1920s, W.O. was offered a substantial price for the property but refused it. In 1953 and 1954, in two separate steps, W.O. and Grace donated the property to the W. O'Neil Foundation, which later sold the gift for about $55,000. But W.O. always maintained that from a strictly financial angle it had been a bad deal "because Grace insisted on going to Florida every year just to look at it."

An interesting sidelight of the 1914 McGraw Tire deal was that E. C. McGraw, in 1917, offered W.O. a contract of $25,000 a year plus 10 per cent of the net profits for ten years to take charge of the McGraw Tire & Rubber Company, which then grossed ten million dollars annually and was financially sound. W.O.'s General Tire & Rubber Company was then in its second year of production. His income was much less than the McGraw offer, but he was not tempted seriously. By then he was building the kind of tire he had discussed with Win Fouse in their after-hours conversations in Kansas City.

5

"I don't want to be a home-talent producer"

Early in 1915, Will O'Neil made a trip back to Akron to disclose to his father his plans to expand the operations of the Western Tire & Rubber Company into the manufacture of tires. The year before, Western had shown net profits of $46,000, which the two young partners had split equally. In addition, each had drawn a salary of $300 a month. Each therefore had an annual income of more than $25,000, a handsome figure. Will, however, had decided that their $500,000 gross business in tire-repair products should anticipate a reduced market, as the evolution of tires made them more dependable and less susceptible to blowouts and punctures. "I knew there were going to be fewer punctures from horseshoe nails anyway. That had already started," Will said.

Many of Will's acquaintances on automobile row and in the Kansas City Club had encouraged him to manufacture tires. Among his close friends the idea of a Kansas City tire generated civic pride. One banker who heard of the embryonic plans expressed this feeling to Will a few days before he decided to return to Akron for a talk with his father. "A great many of your friends will help you by buying stock, Will," the banker said. "And based on Western's past earnings, we can give you a good line of credit. All of us think it would be great to have a tire made here. You will get a lot of support for a home-town tire."

Here was another of those chance remarks which seemed uncannily to set Will O'Neil's mind to pondering more deeply than the remark itself justified. In Denver in 1908, he had been stimulated by the tire distributor's offhand description of Kansas City as "a whale of a territory." The comment had sparked something in Will O'Neil's imagination implying spaciousness, room for action, a large area of unrestricted opportunity. And it had worked out that way. So long as he had plenty of territory as a tire jobber, he had been happy and successful. As the territory was restricted, he had broken the local bonds by venturing into manufacturing. He built a sales organization which spread over a larger territory than Western had originally controlled as a tire jobber.

Now the words that stuck in his mind were the banker's "You'll get a lot of support for a home-town tire." Will was not interested in a local tire. His mind recalled "local talent" plays, and how they were supported by local pride or from a sense of duty by groups within a community. He assessed the technical level of a home-talent production against a professional enterprise and decided he did not want to be a home-talent producer. He was grateful to his Kansas City friends for their loyalty, but the tire he wanted to build could only be constructed by the people who knew rubber and tire design as they did in Akron. Akron was the big league of tires, and that's where Will wanted to be.

[46]

Will's problem, when he returned to discuss the matter with his father, was whether to accept the cooperation offered in Kansas City, or—as he preferred—move Western's operation to Akron, enlist the talents of tire experts, and begin the manufacture of tires there. W.O. knew that the move back to Akron would necessitate financial help. He figured that Western's profits would go a long way toward offsetting the start-up costs.

On the long train ride Will O'Neil knew that he was headed toward the biggest selling job of his life. He hoped, of course, to interest his father in a major role in financing the company. Michael had the money, but was disposed against heavy involvement in tire manufacturing. All his life Michael had been a merchant. He had resisted successfully all temptations to become involved in any of the many rubber companies which had been organized in Akron. Some of them had been successful; the great majority had failed, and all of them had agonized through long worrisome periods.

As long as Will could remember Michael had been apprehensive about the wide swings in crude rubber and cotton prices. A tire manufacturer needed big inventories of both—mostly bought in one year for delivery in tires to dealers the next spring—and rubber and cotton were the most volatile commodities on the market. As a boy Will could remember his father saying, "I want to go to bed at night without worrying about what rubber and cotton prices are going to be in the morning."

Michael was now sixty-four years old. At his age he had little incentive to risk a new enterprise. Just two years earlier he had received one million dollars from the sale of his store. When he had told May Company executives that he had already made a million, he was undoubtedly conservative. His funds were invested mainly in Akron real estate, which was growing in value and, with the new Portage Hotel, the new Ohio Building, and his other commercial buildings, was returning a good income. He was also a large holder of municipal bonds. Michael liked such investments. He knew where he stood. He had no desire for more money, especially if any risk to his large family's security was involved. He also had projected a long-range program of philanthropies he did not wish to jeopardize.

Michael probably still felt that Will had shown poor judgment in not "taking over at the store." At any rate, he definitely believed that Will, still only thirty, was impetuous and "too much in a hurry." Even so, Michael was proud of Will's Kansas City success. He often expressed amazement that a business could be built to gross $500,000 a year in tire-repair materials. "Will is a great salesman," he said, but it is significant that he never gave his son outspoken credit for the genius he demonstrated in the larger aspects of business.

All the talks Will O'Neil and his father had, on this first visit to Akron and on frequent subsequent occasions in 1915, took place in the O'Neil home on West Market Street. Will would not discuss the matter in Michael's new office in the just-completed Ohio Building. The reason, of course, was to avoid any possibility of premature publicity. It was natural for Will to be visiting home, and no rumors started. In fact, the secret was so well kept that a search of Akron newspaper files for the year 1915 reveals no newspaper announcement of the formation of the new company.

Upon returning to Akron, one of Will's first calls was a sentimental visit to the M. O'Neil store. Inside the door he met Nate L. Dauby, president of The May Company, and his brother Jerome, who had become the manager of the Akron store. Will knew them both, and they fell into conversation. After a while Jerome was called away, leaving W.O. and Nate alone. Nate suggested that they go to a private office where they might visit more comfortably. Will accepted. There Nate Dauby came to the point. He believed that his brother had managed the Akron store outstandingly, but he wanted Jerome in Cleveland with him. Had Will ever thought of returning to the department-store business? Will told him that he had no such ideas. Dauby pressed the matter and made Will an offer of $25,000 a year to manage the M. O'Neil Company. It would have been excellent public relations to have Michael O'Neil's son manage the M. O'Neil Company. In declining Will felt that he could trust Nate with his secret and decided to reveal his plans for manufacturing tires.

He had evolved definite ideas about the tire he wanted to build and sell in a new way. His firing-line experience, working with tire dealers, had convinced him that there was a profitable market for a better, higher-priced tire. This required distribution through franchised dealers who were trained, full-time tire men, with exclusive territories, so that they too could make money and not be in competition with a dealer on the opposite corner and others down the street, all with the identical tire. He believed, he said, that rubber chemists and tire designers in Akron were capable of creating more advanced tires than the pricing policies of their companies permitted.

When Will finished, Dauby thought a moment, then said, "Will, you can put me down for ten thousand dollars worth of stock."

Will O'Neil left the store elated. He knew that Nate Dauby's offer would impress his father. There is reason to believe that it did. Michael agreed to assist in the financing, provided that he was not obligated to endorse for the company. This was a reasonable precaution. Michael had large assets and therefore a great deal to lose. Many Akronites had lost heavily by endorsing for companies in which they were interested.

Finally the outline of the new company began to take shape. A capitalization of $200,000 was agreed upon, with Michael and Will holding equal numbers of shares which together would give them control. Will and Win agreed to take $50,000 worth of stock in the new company for their Western Tire & Rubber Company assets. On the basis of Western's earnings, they felt this was a low valuation, but they were enthusiastic about the new company's possibilities, and, in view of the low capitalization, accepted. Actually, the investment in The General Tire & Rubber Company proved a bargain for a business based in a rented building on the outskirts of Kansas City.

The company Will O'Neil organized in Akron is the only one ever to have been privately financed entirely by Akron stockholders. Nate Dauby was not, strictly speaking, from Akron, but he certainly had a big stake in its mercantile life. Included were three prominent Akron men whose German ancestry recalled Ferdinand Schumacher's assistance to Michael O'Neil at a critical time. They were Charles Herberich, Gus Burkhardt, and Carl Dietz. Others who invested were the three who joined the new company in key positions—Charles J. Jahant, Robert Iredell, and Harold B. Pushee.

There was one incident of special interest in the busy days of 1915, when Will was virtually commuting between Kansas City and Akron, before The General Tire & Rubber Company was officially incorporated on September 29. An inkling of W.O.'s activities reached Harvey S. Firestone late in the summer, probably in early August. He sent word to W.O. that he would like to see him. A meeting was arranged. Firestone told W.O. of his intention to start a Canadian company. He described the vast territory north of the border—just beginning to accept the automobile. In view of W.O.'s frequently expressed desire for a large territory, he considered Canada the ideal outlet for W.O.'s ambitions and ability. He concluded by offering W.O. a substantial stock interest in the new company and a handsome salary if he would assume the presidency. But Will O'Neil's plans for his own company were far along.

It is interesting, however, that the security of two exceptionally fine opportunities was offered to Will O'Neil, a man of thirty, one from Nate Dauby and one from Harvey Firestone, and that he preferred to continue with his plans to start the rubber industry's 358th competitive company.

The financing details were well along before Will and Michael gave much consideration to a name for the new venture. In a meeting at the O'Neil home one evening, a decision was almost made to adopt the name of The O'Neil Tire & Rubber Company. Michael mentioned the existence of a small local company called the O'Neil Tire & Protector Company, owned by William O'Neil, no relation, who had married a former cashier in the M. O'Neil Company, Kate Tobin. The word Protector described a type of tire boot in which the firm specialized. Will suggested the alternate, General. Ever since, it has been part of the legend at General Tire that W.O. picked General because it connoted a big company like General Electric Corp., General Motors, General Foods, or General Mills. The only one of these that was then in business was General Electric, which dates from 1892. W.O. seems to have been impressed by General Electric and its reputation, size, and successful pioneering in the electric industry. All his life

Will O'Neil was interested in industries that faced the future; all his later diversifications were made in such fields. In 1915 he equated the tire business with his faith in the future of the automobile and the motor truck.

6

"What no tire maker has ever done before"

THE NUMBER of passenger cars in the United States passed the two-million mark in 1915, and some 900,000 new cars were produced during the year. Optimistic predictions were made of a million-and-a-half-car year in 1916. Actually, this figure was exceeded slightly, boosting the number of cars on the road to more than three and a quarter million. Most of these made standard provisions for at least two spare tires, sportier models up to four. Wells at the base of the front fenders where they joined the running boards accommodated two tires; sometimes two more were strapped on the back. Both locations provided "rolling billboard" advertising value for the brand of tires so displayed.

Spare-tire covers of oilcloth or metal were sold as accessories, but tire dealers opposed them. They encouraged exposing the spares, nakedly and with pride, pointing out that the covers retained moisture and caused the tires to deteriorate.

Bill O'Neil was the first manufacturer to contend that

where excessive moisture accumulated, tires in covers deteriorated faster than they did on the road. He originated a service, first performed by General Tire dealers, which quickly became standard practice in the industry— the "rotating" of tires so that the spare, or spares, were put to work at regular mileage intervals. By visiting the dealer for this rotation service, the owner exposed himself to a sale when replacement tires were needed.

Carrying premium spares without covers became a status symbol which endured for many years. Finally carmakers began to wrap the fenders, front and back, around smaller-diameter wheels so that the tires on the car were obscured. When a single spare was relegated to the darkness of the trunk compartment, an era ended.

But in 1915 tires were a much-in-evidence, much-discussed topic wherever car owners got together. They boasted of their mileage much as early radio enthusiasts boasted of the faraway stations they logged. Each nonskid tread had its own informed public, its own army of enthusiasts and detractors. There were many tire brands to keep the interest high. Next to a car's power plant, its reputation for speed and dependability, no item of the automobile received more attention and discussion than its tires.

No one, not even Bill O'Neil, is on record as predicting that in fifty years automotive registrations would crowd a hundred million passenger cars, trucks, and buses. Nor did he anticipate the millions of rubber-tired farm, mine, and other nonhighway vehicles and machinery invented later. The story of the Kansas City banker comes to mind here. It casts a new light on what may have been in Will's mind behind that "lingering Irish smile," when he refused to be switched from the tire business and said "No" to the car manufacturer's offer of a dealership. He had observed that cars were improving, becoming more reliable and less expensive to buy and operate. The Good Roads Movement had begun to make headway in a coast-to-coast Lincoln Highway then under construction.

The evidence is strong that W.O. realized that as the automobile became practical and better roads increased its range of operation, tire usage would increase tremendously, multiplied both by the greater number of cars and by the more miles each would travel. He foresaw that improved tires would be a factor in the growth of automobile usage and that the manufacture, selling, and servicing of tires would remain separate from the functions of the carmaker and dealer.

In later years, Will O'Neil felt that the improvements in tires had not received the credit they should have for putting America on wheels, but he always had a high regard for the *Encyclopaedia Britannica* because its article on the "Motor Car" said "In America . . . the expansion and growth of the motor car has in large measure proceeded abreast with the building of good roads, development of alloy steels and improvement of tires." W.O. always felt that it was only right to put good tires among the three most important factors, but he wouldn't have put them third.

There was no room, however, in the rubber industry in 1915 for just another tire company. The market was so ebullient, the growth prospects so bright, that many companies rushed into the business of manufacturing tires. Just as there have been more than 1500 makes of automobiles, there were hundreds of tire companies. The number 358 is regarded as reliable. It includes companies with only local and regional sales ambitions. Some of them were strictly stock promotions the sponsors of which never built a tire.

Just as at the turn of the century there were plow factories in practically every small city in the farm belt, so
tire plants sprang up everywhere with the early growth
of the auto industry. But the center of tire manufacturing
activity always was Akron. Interestingly, *The Tire Rate
Book* for May 1917, an industry publication, included a
listing for the Kansas City Tire & Rubber Corporation.
Curiously enough, its headquarters were at Chester, West
Virginia, and the company's advertisement announced a
new tire under the trade name Bull, guaranteed for 4000
miles.

The same issue of *The Tire Rate Book* listed 106 tire
manufacturers with national ambitions. The names of some
of these tires have a certain nostalgic interest:

Brunswick	Racine Horse Shoe
Carspring	Smith Canvas Tread
Double Fabric	Speedway
Dry Climate	Standard Four
Gillette-Safety	Swinehart
Nabob	Thermoid
Perfection	Woodworth Trouble-Proof

The Swinehart tire had a connection with the early history of the O'Neils. Thomas F. Walsh, the brother-in-law,
who had been married in a double ceremony with Michael
in St. John's Cathedral, Cleveland, in 1884, was an early
investor in the Swinehart Company. The venture never
was a real moneymaker and had more than its share of
worrisome periods, as Michael undoubtedly knew from
family conversations. Eventually Tom Walsh lost most of
his life's savings in Swinehart, which had the reputation
of being a "local" tire. The lack of success of the Swinehart tire may have been partly responsible for Michael's
lack of enthusiasm for the tire business.

By 1915 many of the tire companies in Akron had become large. From its founding, The General Tire & Rubber Company faced severe competition. Many of the names that are now only legends of the early automotive era were substantial companies.

General was the last major company to be formed in the industry that has survived. Furthermore, its annual sales have grown to exceed a billion dollars.

General Tire officially set up in business on September 29, 1915. Its inaugural amused the experienced rubber men. They found most amusing the fact that Will O'Neil, Win Fouse, and their three technical experts, Charley Jahant, Production Head; Bob Iredell, Chief Engineer; and Harold Pushee, Chemist, averaged thirty years, exactly Will's age. This invariably was offered as proof that the enterprise was brash and ridiculously audacious. "Not one of 'em is old enough to be a General," became the oft-quoted saying of one competitor.

It is worth noting that, perhaps more than any other dynamic growth industry in America—certainly among those leaders with annual sales now in excess of a billion dollars—General Tire is a living corporate example of the creativity, energy, common sense, and talent for leadership in large affairs young men in America are capable of contributing to a business. All the young men who joined General Tire at its founding, and a very high percentage of the original dealers, continued with the company until their retirement years. But young men, two or three or even ten rungs down the ladder, have never been impeded because of that. The way has always been found to utilize all the talent and enthusiasm each ambitious young man had, and to reward him accordingly. This has always been true of General Tire, and W.O. boasted of it frequently. Part of his later interest in diversification was inspired by the opportunities diversification provided to advance younger men in the organization into wider fields and positions of greater responsibility.

"One of the greatest wastes in any company," Bill O'Neil said, "comes from not being able to utilize all the brains and enthusiasms in the organization. We make a mistake when we think that, because of youth, a man has only energy and enthusiasm. Very often he not only has new ideas but also good judgment. General Tire owes its success, basically, to people who have been here for a long time, but it owes a great deal of its growth to the ideas and enthusiasm of people who are too young to remember much about when tires were made of natural rubber."

The three key men who were persuaded by Will O'Neil to join General each invested a few thousand dollars in the venture. Years later, these modest investments had made them wealthy, but all had contributed much more to General's success than their dollars.

Charles J. Jahant, who originated General's production, had been Firestone's Tire Division Superintendent. As boys, he and Will O'Neil had been classmates at the St. Vincent parochial school. When Will left for Holy Cross, Charley remained in Akron, where his father had a hardware store, to attend Buchtel College, now Akron University. After receiving his degree in 1909, Charley joined Firestone, working eleven hours a night for fifteen cents an hour. Many times he wondered whether getting a college education had been worthwhile from an economic standpoint. He made some progress, however. In addition to being superintendent of production, he had acquired about two thousand dollars worth of Firestone stock when his old schoolmate persuaded him to take the big uncertain step into General's future.

Robert Iredell, Charley Jahant's right hand at Firestone,

also decided to go along. He too was from an old Akron family, his grandfather having been the city's first mayor. Like Jahant, he had been graduated from Buchtel, then had received a degree in chemical engineering from the University of Pennsylvania in 1911. Bob had about five thousand dollars to contribute to the new company's capitalization, and a valuable knowledge of tire engineering.

Charley Jahant was elected to the board of directors in 1929, Bob Iredell in 1941. Both remained directors after officially retiring; Jahant as Vice-President in Charge of Production and Iredell as Director of Engineering.

Harold B. Pushee, the only non-Akronite among the original five, was a native of Woburn, Massachusetts, and a graduate of Massachusetts Institute of Technology. He was only twenty-five when General Tire was organized, but had already demonstrated his knowledge of rubber chemistry at another Akron company. Hearing of Will O'Neil's plans, he offered his talents. Like the others, his savings of a few thousand dollars were also invested and he began a career that made many contributions to General's success.

Pushee is the only one whose exact date of employment with the company is known—September 4, 1915—a little more than three weeks before the enterprise was officially incorporated.

The Akron *Beacon Journal* included a historical piece on The General Tire & Rubber Company in a special edition of the paper published to celebrate Akron's hundredth birthday in 1925, when General was just ten years old. The article said, in part:

> The General Tire & Rubber Company has been a success story from the beginning . . . it reads a little differently from the story of other companies hereabouts. In 1915 the

city of Akron offered [General] no bonus and none was asked. There was no invitation from the Chamber of Commerce and none was expected. There were no subsidies, no special financing. . . .

The East Akron site selected for the factory was 'way out in the country. East Market Street was not paved that far; there was no city water; the plant was a half mile from the end of the car line. . . .

In manufacturing and sales, General launched policies that were strange to the industry and were laughed at by competitors. . . . The company's strength lies in the excellence of its products and in the standing of its dealers.

As the organizer of the company, Will O'Neil chose his father to be President and himself to be Vice-President and General Manager. Although he headed the company from the start, W.O. did not assume the presidency until 1924. The other original officers in 1915 were Charles Herberich, Treasurer, and Win Fouse, Secretary.

During its first year, General Tire employed approximately a hundred people, the same number Western employed in Kansas City. Most of them continued with General for many years. They possessed great *esprit de corps*. Many of them were highly individualistic and left the comparative security of jobs with major rubber companies because of stories they had heard about General and its colorful and highly informal leader, Bill O'Neil. Here was a place a man could enjoy his work, and be proud of what he did.

One of the first of this breed to be hired was Andrew J. Halter. Andy was credited with building the first pneumatic tire, while he was employed at the B. F. Goodrich Company. An Akron boy, he joined Goodrich in 1884. A few years later, Andy was put in charge of developing a strange new product—a tire filled with air. The development was a success, and Andy became what Akron knows as a Development Man.

In 1905, Andy left Goodrich for similar work at the Republic Rubber Company, then located in Youngstown, Ohio. Eleven years later, hearing of the formation of General Tire, he decided to apply for a job. He loved to tell what happened. He had returned to Akron for a visit. Through a friend he learned that General sought a man with his experience. The friend offered to make an appointment for him with Bill O'Neil. The next day Andy appeared at the General plant, only to be told by someone that there were no vacancies. Assuming that his friend had failed in the effort to make an appointment for him, Andy returned to Youngstown.

Later, W.O. dispatched an emissary to Youngstown to locate him. As an employee of General, Andy supervised the construction of a tire the company viewed with pride. Among other talents, Andy could tell how well rubber was cured by biting a piece of it. This ability was the more mysterious because he wore full dentures. In view of the computerized research and development that was to come, this was a primitive beginning. As graduate scientists and laboratory methods were adopted, Andy proudly relied on his experience, instinct, and knowledge to guide him through the maze of intricate development. He loved to jab at the more sophisticated technical men with one of his favorite taunts: "I just out-know you."

One day the production and development people had decided upon a particular procedure, and W.O. asked Andy for his opinion.

" 'Twon't work," Andy grunted.

"Why?"

" 'Tain't no good," was the reply.

"Why's it no good?" W.O. persisted.

" 'Cause it won't work," said Andy. And that was that.

But the plan was followed, and a few days later a report went to W.O. The idea was no good, because it wouldn't work; and it seemed the reason it wouldn't work was that it was no good.

Andy died in 1940, his reputation secure as a real pioneer of the rubber industry in the nineteenth century. During his many years with General he made outstanding contributions to the development of modern balloon tires for both passenger cars and trucks.

The new factory and office buildings were scarcely under cover in September 1915. Calenders, mills, and other rubber-working machinery had been ordered. Some had not yet arrived, others needed assembling. Jahant, Iredell, and Pushee pitched in with the hourly employees to establish production. The first objective was to duplicate in Akron the manufacturing of repair materials done in Kansas City. It had been part of Will O'Neil's original plans for these repair items to carry the costs until the new company's tire was available. This program was followed. General's sales in the first year amounted to $219,197, yielding a profit of $620. So the venture did not start in the red, the only tire company in Akron with that record.

Experiments with a new tire were carried on through the first nine months of 1916, when production of the first General tire was achieved. The product was a beauty for its day, with a distinctive, rich-looking, pearl-gray sidewall. The tread was original, too, with a continuous center rib for smooth riding, and deep nonskid markings on either side. Charley Jahant and his men had done their work well.

W.O. knew he could sell it. It *looked* like a better tire. It had the best of materials in it, and careful workmanship. Best of all, it was not an "iron tire." Slightly oversized in cross section but with rim dimensions that made it fit standard rims, it was a long step toward proving the better riding qualities of a large-cross-section tire. This was the industry's first oversize tire—the forerunner of the low-pressure cord tire which General pioneered in 1920—and actually lifted the curtain on development leading eventually to modern low-pressure balloon tires.

It was only a part of W.O.'s philosophy to have a top-quality tire with a distinctive appearance. The next essential was to surround it with an aura of prestige, so that people would recognize it instinctively as a better tire and be willing to pay for the difference. This involved prestige advertising on a national scale, not only to sell the public but also—and more important—to attract responsible businessmen to take the General Tire franchise in their cities on an exclusive territorial basis, in return for a modest investment in inventory and full-time devotion to selling and servicing General tires.

W.O.'s only semblance of a dealer organization was the old Western Tire & Rubber Company's sales force in Kansas City. It continued to sell the repair materials after their manufacture was transferred to Akron, and gradually was converted to a regular General Tire dealership. Other dealers were found in the area and, for the first two years of General Tire's existence, the volume of business in the Kansas City section was five times the volume of the Ohio section. W.O. always said he never knew whether he should be proud of this, but nevertheless it was a fact, and it was a great help to the establishment of the infant company.

The big problem was how to attract a nationwide dealer organization. What W.O. needed most was an impressive national advertising campaign, which even then was expensive. At that time, *The Saturday Evening Post* was the undisputed national advertising medium, "the showplace of American industry," particularly favored by automotive advertisers. A black-and-white page cost five thousand dollars. Other tire companies, including the largest, were using fractional pages, and only occasionally a full page. W.O. wanted to run full pages only. These would make General appear as big as its largest competitor. Impressive size and well-conceived copy would give to General the prestige image O'Neil desired. He visualized five full-page ads in the *Post* as the minimum necessary to attract eligible dealers to inquire about franchises. Unfortunately, the company checks were signed by Michael as president. Will knew that any proposal to spend $25,000 on an advertising campaign in the *Post* would be opposed by his father. Moreover, he had no ad layouts or copy that satisfied him; two leading agencies had failed to impress him.

As W.O.'s first association with Win Fouse or his conversation with Nate Dauby or his choice of Jahant, Iredell, and Pushee might be considered fortuitous, the solution of his advertising problem carried the same stamp of opportunity sought and seized. In the smoking compartment of a train from New York, W.O. found himself seated next to a tall, impeccable young man with the impressive name of J. Ferdinand Oberwinder, a young advertising executive with the D'Arcy Advertising Company of St. Louis. It was impossible for Will O'Neil to sit next to anyone for any length of time without starting a conversation, and equally impossible for Ferd Oberwinder not to listen when he scented an advertising account in search of a home.

W.O. described his quality tire and exclusive-dealer philosophy in some detail; also his advertising hopes. Oberwinder saw a link between the General Tire franchise plan and the Coca-Cola system; D'Arcy had created the

Coco-Cola account from its beginning. W.O. was impressed by Oberwinder and by what he told him of the D'Arcy advertising philosophy. All D'Arcy accounts were premium-priced products. Coca-Cola sold for a nickel, as did all other soft drinks, but in a six-ounce bottle, considerably smaller than any competitor's. Another client, Budweiser Beer, was a nickel a bottle more expensive than any other. The two men scheduled a meeting in Akron, where Oberwinder would receive the necessary information, and D'Arcy would prepare a campaign.

The ads were prepared. Now all W.O. had to do was get the money. One legend reports that W.O., recognizing that his brother Tom was his father's favorite, appointed him director of advertising before the crucial meeting with Michael. Tom explained the plan in Michael's office. "What does it cost?" Quickly W.O. replied, "Five thousand dollars." Michael thought he meant five thousand for the five ads, excessive for a $200,000 company; but finally he agreed reluctantly. The two sons left the office immediately.

Because of the delay in publishing suitable advertising, the first General Tire ad did not run in the *Post* until January 27, 1917. It was entirely different from any other tire advertising of the era.

The heading was WHAT NO TIRE-MAKER HAS EVER DONE BEFORE. At the bottom was a picture of the new pearl-gray sidewall General tire, exposed on its side across the entire page, with impressive factories depicted in the hole in the center, a large signature reading *The General Tire*, and a prominent declaration: *Built in Akron*.

The text of this first ad read:

We've established throughout the United States, in a year's time, a tire success from every standpoint of performance, popularity and sales—established it with distributor, dealer and user. The General tire stands out as the tire that stands up.

And we've done what no tire-maker has ever done before, because we did in the first place what no tire-maker had ever done before.

When we started, we knew what tire users wanted and needed—we knew how to make that kind of tire and we had the will to make it.

We had no old methods of our own to cling to through sentiment, stubbornness or economy. We had no old machinery or equipment that we had to get along with.

We had no past of our own to handicap us and we did have the pasts and presents of others to warn us of pitfalls in tire-making.

In Akron we built a factory equipped with the very last word in tire-making and perfecting machinery.

As you know, Akron is the center of the tire brains of the world. We located the best of the tire brains in Akron and the world and put them to work in carrying out our ideals.

When you put to work the knowledge of a need—the know-how to fulfill that need—the machinery, equipment and materials to produce the results demanded by the know-how —the brains to see that results are produced, and the will to make a good tire, you can't make anything but a good tire.

There's the whole reason for the success of The General Tire—unvarying quality produced by building into it the best of Akron and the best of ourselves.

Now—after reading this, you are expecting the General to be a high-priced tire. Just ask the dealer and be surprised at how moderate the price is. And as to cost in service—the General costs less per guaranteed mile.

This first General Tire advertisement attracted many letters from prospective dealers. No one now recalls just how many. But the nucleus of a national dealer organization was created out of inquiries from this and the subsequent *Post* ads. Bill O'Neil also had his own personal and inimitable way of selecting dealers. A few others were chosen from among salesmen who solicited General in these early days, particularly if they happened to call at an odd hour: early in the morning, or on Saturday, or after closing time. W.O. had already formed his habit of roaming the offices. When few of his own people were on hand, he sought out and talked to any outside salesmen who appeared. Many of the original franchises are still operated by the sons of the original owners.

A good example of recruiting is the case of Howard Bischoff, for more than forty years the very successful Cincinnati dealer before he retired. Early one Saturday morning in February 1918 Howard, who was the Akron salesman for a Cincinnati paper firm, made a routine call at the General offices. He saw the advertising manager, Ben Stiller, who had been with W.O. in Kansas City in a similar capacity. Stiller needed some letterheads, invoices, and envelopes on which young Bischoff quoted a price of $360. This was less than Stiller had been paying, but a purchase of that size required W.O.'s approval. Suddenly W.O. appeared at the door, whereupon Stiller introduced Bischoff and asked for the O.K. But first, W.O. wanted to talk about something else. He sat down, stretched his long legs, and after a moment of silence said: "You mean you're a salesman, Mr. Bischoff, and you work on Saturday?" A brief, bantering conversation followed, after which O'Neil accepted the order. He then offered Bischoff a franchise in Buffalo and invited him to lunch, in that order and in a very few moments.

"The entire conversation didn't take five minutes," Bischoff recalled later, "but I accepted the invitation to lunch, and on the ride to the restaurant, Mr. O'Neil again brought up the opening in Buffalo. I told him that I could not possibly consider moving there. That if I were to move from Akron, it would have to be back to my home town of Cincinnati. I told him that I was only twenty-two, had been married less than a year, and with all bills paid, was probably worth about two hundred dollars. This recital did not discourage him and as we entered the restaurant, he was still painting a glowing picture of the opportunities that General offered its dealers. Sometime during the lunch, I tentatively agreed to try to raise a few thousand dollars capital, and the upshot was that I became the dealer in Cincinnati a short time later and never had the slightest reason to regret it. The business prospered greatly over the years, and one of the great satisfactions was the privilege of working with Will O'Neil. I never knew why he offered me a dealership so soon after we met that Saturday morning back in 1918. I guess he was just naturally attracted to any salesman who worked on Saturday morning."

Another young man appeared at the General Tire plant early in 1919. He had been a military pilot, a Signal Corps partner of Jimmy Doolittle's in air battles over France in World War I. Now he wanted to enter the tire business with General, preferably in California. His name was Dan A. Kimball, whose career with General and in government service was to be long and distinguished. But no red rug was rolled out for him the day he applied in Akron.

"I must have arrived at a conventional hour of the day or something," Kimball recalls. "I didn't meet Will O'Neil, and Sam Poor, who interviewed me, didn't hold out much hope. I told him that I was on my way to California because my mother was there, and not in good health. He took my mother's address and promised to get in touch with me if anything opened up. A week later, when I arrived at my mother's, a wire was waiting offering me a job if I would report to the manager of General's Los Angeles branch. I don't remember how long it took but it was quite a while before it dawned on me that the man I talked to in Akron saw no point in hiring me there and have the company pay my expenses to California, since I was coming out anyway."

From this frosty "welcome aboard," Kimball went on to become General's Western sales manager until, in 1941, he was appointed to head General's Washington offices. He was a vice-president and director of General before resigning in 1949 to become, successively, Assistant Secretary of the Navy for Air, Under-Secretary of the Navy and, in 1951, Secretary. He returned to General in 1953 as vice-president and director.

7

"Why didn't you just ask him to change a five?"

THE General Tire & Rubber Company would have been an entirely different kind of company had it not been for Grace O'Neil. Will had a compulsive attitude toward his work and delegated very little of it, particularly during the years he was creating his company. There was so much to be done, with never enough hours in the day. He might easily have exhausted himself physically, especially in view of his medical history. Grace helped him keep his activities in perspective. More than anyone else, she helped him to humanize General Tire, and no quality of the company contributed more to its success than that.

Grace O'Neil was the chief influence in establishing a big informal family of General Tire and its dealers. She did this not so much in a conscious effort to make a success of the business as to ease Will's burdens.

Creating the atmosphere of a big family, and enjoying it, came easily to Grace. When Will had met her in Kansas City, she was one of the eight Savage children, five girls and three boys, whose home was a hospitality center for the friends of all of them—John, Jr., Grace, Patricia, Lucida, Kathleen, Margaret, James, and Frank. Her father was a native of Lexington, Kentucky, who became a general contractor in Kansas City. Many of the bridges in northwestern Kansas, which only recently have begun to be skirted or supplanted by freeways, were built by John Savage. His wife, before her marriage, had been Susan McMennimen, born in Kansas City to a pioneer family and reared there amid a host of relatives and friends. Susan could never understand how her daughter could be happy moving as far east as Akron, Ohio.

Grace's older brother John was a well-known young Kansas Citian and an early friend of W.O. He was business manager of the Kansas City Blues, then in the American Association and owned by George Tebeau, in whose motor-row car agency Grace was working when Will met her. Many of the baseball stars of the era dropped in frequently to see Tebeau, some to get a discount on a Stearns automobile, some just to talk baseball. Grace became a great fan, and has remained one all her life. She knew Casey Stengel, who used to drop in at the agency, and must be one of the few women in the country who knows that the nickname Casey derives from *K. C.* Grace is also authority for the fact that Stengelese, that rambling sentence structure he highly publicized in later years, was not in evidence then at contract-signing time. He spoke very clearly and to the point. Much later, after Grace and Will had moved to Akron, the National League pennant, in 1925, was won by Pittsburgh and Grace drove to attend every World Series game played there. She is still a great Pirate fan.

One way Grace O'Neil helped to inject an unusually tangible family spirit into the early General Tire & Rubber Company was a direct result of W.O.'s disregard for time.

Dealers visiting in his office frequently found themselves still there at seven-thirty or eight o'clock in the evening, usually as unaware of time as was W.O. Then W.O. would reach for his desk telephone and call his home. "Grace, what are we having for dinner tonight? I've got Jim Campbell and Joe Grady in the office, and I thought we'd come out." Campbell was the very successful General dealer in Pittsburgh; Grady was the same in Syracuse, New York. W.O. might forget to mention one or two others he picked up as he left the building. Such conduct was routine. It never mattered how much later than the normal Akron dinner hour this happened, or how often; Grace accepted it as a happy if abnormal way of life. She knew most of the dealers, their wives, their children by names and ages, where they attended school, and—likely as not—how well each was doing. Much too youthful to be a matriarch, Grace was the warm-hearted mother of a growing family during this period and shared the life of the dealers' families more intimately than any mere business relationship could engender.

Jim Campbell, the Pittsburgh dealer, was a classmate of O'Neil's at Holy Cross. A successful salesman and a fan of the Pirates, Jim was especially welcome in the O'Neil household around training season, as he brought the latest gossip on Grace's favorite baseball team. Jim once recalled asking Grace, "Doesn't it bother you, Grace, to have Will call up at eight o'clock to say he's bringing out dealers for dinner?" "Not at all," Grace replied with her sly smile. "It's much better than when he doesn't call."

The year of General's first million-dollar profit, 1923, was also a highlight in the home life of the O'Neils. In May the only daughter joined the family of five brothers and was christened Grace after her mother. Bill was ten, Tom eight, John six, Hugh four, and Michael Gerald—

already responding only to the name Jerry, which clung to him ever after—was a year and a half.

Curiously, the children were alternately blue-eyed and brown-eyed, starting with Bill whose eyes were blue and ending with Grace whose eyes were a lovely, soft brown. W.O. claimed he planned the family that way. "It made it easier to tell them apart," he would explain. His own blue eyes would twinkle while Grace regarded him with a hazel-eyed glance which indicated clearly that he assumed too much credit in the matter. The ocular characteristic among the children was recognized by all of them at an early age. In choosing up sides for childish games, they lost no time in deciding on teams. The Blues competed against the Browns. This meant that Bill, John, and Jerry played Tom, Hugh, and Grace. The phenomenon also caused Grace, who became Mrs. William Mahon Regan of New York City, to be extremely conscious of the color of people's eyes. Even now, she has a distinctive ability to recall the color of eyes of those she has met— perhaps only casually—years ago. W.O. used to say hers was a mental trick "like remembering license numbers."

W.O. chose the jubilant year of 1923 to build a beautiful Tudor home on West Exchange Street, as a gift to Grace and to provide room for the family which had grown almost as fast as the business. Until that time the family had moved every few years as new arrivals dictated the need for another bedroom.

The new O'Neil home was completed late that summer. Set on beautifully landscaped grounds, the house occupied a corner in what is still a neighborhood of quietly elegant homes in Akron. In fact, the neighborhood is probably quieter now than when the five O'Neil brothers built low-cost housing projects in the trees and played rounders in the yard with their friends. The fad of improvising swings by hanging discarded tires from tree limbs was just beginning. But W.O. refused to let his sons use an old General. "Any tire is good enough for that," he told them, and the next night brought home a worn-out casing of another make.

When the new O'Neil home was completed, Akron neighbors were amazed by its size and elegance. W.O.'s habits were simple. He spent little money and had never quite outgrown the habit of buying department-store suits that "nobody else wanted." As far as the neighbors could see, the family until then had lived in a style appropriate to the $300-a-month salary O'Neil allowed himself. On this amount Grace had maintained a charming home—with plenty of children—despite W.O.'s occasional whimsical purchase of a $450 Victrola or some other relative nonessential and veto of a rug, davenport, or some other item Grace needed. His defense for impulsive luxury buying such as a Victrola was that the purchase would "please Grace."

The new home was quite a responsibility for Grace to manage, and she decided that she required a bit more financial independence. W.O. then gave Grace a checkbook, but even this financial maneuver turned out well for him. Some of the first checks Grace wrote were to buy Will better clothes.

The spacious house permitted Will to entertain more dealers at dinner. The party was perfect if the dealers played bridge. Then W.O. might enjoy his only nonbusiness pastime and talk some business, too. Grace was an exceptionally good player. Usually W.O. did well with a system which involved what he called "psychic bidding." He preferred partners who knew that he was inclined to overbid.

As a young man, W.O. did much serious reading. Later

[74]

he became a Western buff. Long before Westerns had become popular on television, he devoured them with the voracious appetite of a mystery-story addict.

To his sons, W.O. recommended James Fenimore Cooper, especially *The Pathfinder* and *The Deerslayer*. As an indication that his Irish ancestry had left its cultural impact, W.O. was familiar with the scant output of the Irish writer Gerald Griffin, whom he recommended to his sons. Griffin was born in 1803, in Limerick, Ireland, and died at the age of thirty-seven as a London newspaperman. His serious work included minor poetry, a number of short stories of Irish life, one successful play, and a novel, *The Collegians*. The source of W.O.'s admiration for Griffin is not known. The author had been dead for nearly ninety years when W.O. recommended him to his sons, and never had many enthusiasts. O'Neil must have found in Griffin's works a discernible and worthwhile "difference."

On the subject of W.O.'s Irish ancestry, it is fairly well known that in the colorful years that lay ahead for him, newsmagazines and feature writers invariably referred to his antecedents. *Time* magazine once called him "a professional Irishman." Naturally, W.O. did not like this phrase, but he pretended that he had never heard it and did not know what it meant. He enjoyed asking people around the company to define the phrase, and was delighted that no two definitions were alike. The one that amused him most was offered by a third-generation Akronite whose name was prefixed by *von*. "I'll tell you, W.O., a professional Irishman is one who keeps the *O* in front of his name a hundred years after the family comes over."

In the late 1920s, W.O. developed a fondness for the movies. On the evenings he arrived home at a normal

Akron dinner hour—if no visiting dealers accompanied him—he read briefly after eating and generally fell asleep in his chair. He awoke as if by an alarm clock just in time to round up members of the family old enough to stay awake for the second show, which began at nine-thirty. This phase lasted well into the 1930s. In fact, there is a story that the family habit ended after W.O. awoke from his nap one evening, calling Grace to round up the children for the movie. "We are here alone," Grace said simply. "All the children have dates." So Grace and W.O. attended the movie alone.

W.O.'s son John remembers that the mad dashes in the car to reach the second show on time happened at least twice a week for a long time. Sometimes the drive was more exciting than the movie, because W.O. drove with the intensity and singleness of purpose of an offensive tackle. He never had a serious accident (a fact he attributed modestly to using General tires at all times), but there were those who thought the company would have been wise to provide him a chauffeur long before it did. Such a maneuver would have been impracticable, however, because no one drove to suit W.O.—except his wife Grace—any more than his driving suited anyone else, including his wife Grace.

W.O.'s idiosyncrasies with respect to his car extended to the parking. He never locked his vehicle. "When you lock a car, all you lock out is yourself" was his dictum on this subject. In later years, to leave an automobile unlocked became illegal in many states. W.O. regarded this as an invasion of his property rights and a distinct restriction of his personal liberty.

As a matter of fact, W.O. held a dim view of all locks and keys, probably because his movements were impulsive. His temperament was irritated by a struggle with balky keys. He said once that the first lock was "invented by an only child." He pretended, at least, to believe that if locks had never been invented there would have been less thievery. "It never would have got started," he claimed.

Nevertheless, Grace always insisted that the house doors be locked when the family retired. Will recalled that at lockup time his father said, "I remember that in Ireland no one ever locked a door." In view of the fact that his father had arrived in this country before he was a year old, Will credited him with a remarkable memory indeed.

The drives to the movies, with W.O. at the wheel, were unforgettably exciting to the children. But in contrast to their hectic pace was the leisure of summer trips when their mother drove. These were long cross-country tours, usually to Kansas City, where they went every summer, including the year in which Grace's parents celebrated their fiftieth wedding anniversary. Once they drove to New York City, twice to Niagara Falls.

It was unusual then for a woman driver to undertake trips of this kind, especially with six children. But Grace enjoyed them greatly and so, of course, did the children. The Blues and the Browns had a game they played as their mother motored through the countryside. Each team counted the horses on one side of the road or the other. Each brown or dappled horse counted one point. Sometimes the scores were quite high, and the excitement and concentration of the children became intense. The fun had a thrilling climax: the appearance of a white or gray horse canceled the score of the unlucky team on whose side it appeared and ended the contest in favor of the other team. Playing this game over and over consumed hours, and Grace was always grateful for the day she had devised it.

These cross-country trips gave Grace an opportunity to visit the General Tire dealer in the towns through which she passed. She liked to do this, especially if he was not well known to her. A kindly person herself, she believed that people liked to do small favors. She formed a habit of asking the favor of cashing a small check. Many of the men Grace met in this way she later entertained in her home when they came to Akron.

One evening after dinner while still seated at the table, one of these dealers mentioned that he had first met Mrs. O'Neil by cashing her check. Grace then explained a little of her philosophy about how she felt that people like to do small favors for others. W.O., who seemed not to be paying attention, suddenly asked, "Why didn't you just ask him to change a five-dollar bill?"

The small hazards of entertaining customers in a home where there are small children were lived through. At dinner one night in 1930 was Howard Bischoff, the Cincinnati dealer. With him was a very important customer, the purchasing director of Procter & Gamble. Howard sought to interest his guest in a national contract for the tires on all Procter & Gamble cars throughout the United States.

Gleaming bars of Ivory Soap were in all the bathrooms in the O'Neil home when the guests arrived. After cocktails, as the party was about to move to the dining room, seven-year-old Grace called down the stairs, "Mommy, may I use the new cake of pretty white soap now?"

Back at Cincinnati, Howard got the contract.

8

"Shoes can't blow out
and kill you"

THE YEAR 1920 is remembered in Akron as
1665 is recalled in London, as the time of the great plague.
Spirits were high as the year opened. It seemed like another record-breaking year. More than 1.9 million cars
were manufactured, and nearly 350,000 trucks. Such production should have meant extremely good times for
Akron, especially for the big manufacturers making equipment tires. The replacement market for tires had broadened as total vehicle registrations approached the 10-mil-
lion figure: about 8.5 million cars and 1.5 million trucks.

But there were small signs of trouble as the year opened.
The money market tightened and the prices of commodities basic to the tire business were high, cotton in particular. The price of long-staple cotton advanced from a dollar a pound, a high price, early in the year, to two and a
half. Will O'Neil was concerned. He had been prudent
and conservative in his cotton purchases and was in no
trouble. But General's sales improved every month. Had
he built up a large enough inventory? How much higher

could cotton prices go? Was this a permanent new high plateau for cotton prices, making three or even four-dollar cotton a possibility in the future? W.O.'s five-year-old company had earned a profit every year. This record was unique in Akron history, and W.O. did not want it destroyed, especially in a year of good sales opportunities. "I had the feeling we were building tires out of quicksilver instead of rubber and cotton," W.O. said.

He approached his problem directly. He sought out his friend Frank Seiberling, president of Goodyear, for an opinion on the situation. Seiberling gave it, directly and forcibly. "Don't buy cotton in today's market, Bill. Prices are too high, and are sure to come down. A high market or a low one is never permanent." W.O. took this advice and, largely because of it, avoided the troubles which shook, and in some cases wrecked, the other rubber companies in Akron in late 1920 and 1921.

In July, Harvey Firestone left for England with his family to live as a country squire for three months in a rented Sussex manor house. He was summoned home by cable in early September. The cotton market had collapsed, and crude rubber had dropped from fifty-five cents a pound to sixteen cents. Firestone's inventory shrank $35 million in value. The company's bank loans totaled $43 million. Upon his arrival in Akron, Firestone's first move was to announce a 25 per cent slash in tire prices. This cut was announced in a huge advertising campaign. Resultant sales raised $18 million in cash for Firestone in two months. The sales eased Firestone's credit situation, but the drastic price cut compounded the troubles of the other tire companies, especially those of the big equipment-tire manufacturers.

Goodyear was so severely hurt that in May 1921 the company was taken over by its bank creditors, and Frank Seiberling was retired, along with his brother Charles.

Akron legend asserts that Frank Seiberling's trouble at Goodyear originated in his policy of continuing to buy high-priced cotton all through 1920. Will O'Neil never believed this rumor. As president of the company, Seiberling should have known of the excessive inventory, but W.O. was always convinced that the purchases were made without Seiberling's knowledge.

That's how the Roaring Twenties began in Akron—with a year of boom and bust. All of the tire companies without exception suffered as the value of their inventories plummeted, and those with big bank loans on their inventories found themselves in deep trouble. W.O. piloted his company safely around the inventory reef, but there were two financial transactions that made the dark days of 1920 memorable for him.

General had placed $2.8 million in commercial paper with a Chicago financial house which was underwriting the issue. During the crisis the paper became relatively unmarketable and the underwriter was forced to hold it temporarily for his own account. At this time General's maximum line of credit with any individual banking house was in the neighborhood of $300,000, and here was one house holding nine or ten times that amount. W.O. hopped a train to Chicago and in a brief meeting convinced the underwriters they had nothing to fear . . . and the company later paid off on schedule.

Flushed with this triumph, W.O. headed for New York, where General had what W.O. regarded as a routine note for $250,000 with the National City Bank of New York, which has since loaned The General Tire & Rubber Company many millions of dollars. In the office of William S. Lambie, the bank's vice-president in charge of General's account, W.O. learned to his consternation that the bank had decided not to renew the note. With a few well-chosen and explosive words, W.O. wrote a check for the full amount and walked out.

By coincidence that same afternoon Sam Poor, General's sales manager, was trying to sell the General change-over plan to Uppercue Cadillac of New York, the largest Cadillac dealer in the country. To the Uppercue people, General was a small little-known rubber company away out in Akron, Ohio. Its management wanted references. Sam Poor suggested a call to the National City Bank. Lambie was reached within an hour of W.O.'s visit to his office. Without a moment's hesitation he said, "I think they're going places."

This was the beginning of a very profitable Cadillac changeover business for General Tire in New York. The friendship between O'Neil and Lambie grew. Until Lambie's retirement as senior vice-president of the bank, W.O. seldom went to New York without calling at his office for a friendly visit. There were a number of New York bankers in this category—men W.O. called on almost every time he went to New York.

General survived the crisis year of 1920 with impressive vitality. Profits were trimmed considerably but, compared to most of the others, the little five-year-old company "'way out in the country" was a beacon of stability. Net profits, after taxes, were $81,312. To bring this figure into perspective, here is the profit picture for the first five years:

1916	$ 620
1917	110,877
1918	152,510
1919	376,132
1920	81,312

The total for the five years—$721,351—amounted to more than three and a half times the company's original capitalization, notwithstanding the abnormalities of 1920. Of course, new capital had had to be added, but the record was nonetheless outstanding and this record did not escape the attention of the other rubber companies. Big competitors no longer were amused by Will O'Neil's unconventional ideas about the tire business. All of them were geared to high-volume production, based on the original-equipment business of the automobile manufacturers. None concerned itself with the market for what competitors liked to call "Bill O'Neil's innovations." On the other hand, O'Neil concerned himself solely with selling his "cost more—worth more" tire to individual car owners through franchised dealers with exclusive territories, backed generously by distinctive advertising. General had neither the production facilities for high-volume contract sales to car manufacturers nor the capital to buy the huge inventories of rubber and cotton at least six months in advance which would have been required for original-equipment sales.

General's profit in 1920 was clipped also by the expense of introducing a "Bill O'Neil innovation"—the first General Jumbo tire. This tire, as its name indicates, was oversize in cross section but fit the standard rims of the day. It was a step toward W.O.'s idea that tires should take greater advantage of rubber's resilience and run long mileages with lower air pressures. The Jumbo was an instant success with dealers and the public. It was the first low-pressure cord tire, and embodied several design and construction features that made the modern balloon tire not merely possible but inevitable. The quality and design "difference" established the "Change-Over to General" program, so successful with three generations of tire buyers.

[83]

The Jumbo "put more rubber on the road"—one of the things W.O. in his Kansas City days had decided should be done. It ran more quietly and was more skid-resistant. It gave excellent mileage, the one thing other manufacturers claimed a low-pressure tire could not do. It should be remembered that car owners of this era placed tremendous store by, and boasted about, the number of miles they could coax from their tires. It was their one yardstick of value. W.O. recognized this, and his first slogan for General was "Goes a Long Way to Make Friends." This appeared in General Tire advertising as early as 1918. Not many years later, he was advertising "It's the second 10,000 miles that makes the big hit."

For the most part, however, this mileage advertising was defensive. Mileage was the Johnny-one-note theme of all tire advertising. To justify its higher price, General had to strike an occasional blow for it, but W.O.'s heart was never in mileage claims. It was one of the frustrations of his life that he could never get people to apply what he liked to call "human mileage" rather than speedometer miles to their estimation of tire value.

He never understood why a prosperous, prudent business or professional man—especially a man with a family—took pride in trying to get the last few thousand miles from a set of tires. "It's foolish and dangerous," he said. "Ninety per cent of all the trouble people have with tires comes from trying to get the last ten per cent of possible wear out of them. Why do they do it? They don't do it with their car. They don't even do it with a pair of shoes—and shoes can't blow out and kill you."

Nineteen twenty-three, as mentioned, was the first year in which General Tire profits, after taxes, passed the million-dollar mark. On sales totaling about 8.5 million dollars, a net profit of $1,014,180 was realized. It is not hard to imagine Bill O'Neil's pleasure and satisfaction over this result. It was a remarkable record for a company that had begun just eight years earlier in an industry of giants, with a capitalization of only $200,000 and with a philosophy and methodology that ran completely counter in many ways to the successful formulae of its competition. The company's shares were split two for one and a stock dividend of 100 per cent was voted. This reflects O'Neil's optimism over his first million-dollar year.

But O'Neil was never satisfied with the *status quo*. He lived in a world animated by his own ideas and had the unlimited, restless energy—and the courage—either to try them out or to change his mind next morning and try something else.

W.O. loved to "reverse the field" with ideas exactly the opposite of his conventional competition. More often than not this gambit paid off brilliantly. A good example was the advertising campaign he launched after the announcement of General Tire's first million-dollar year.

It sounded almost like a retrenchment program. Every trade magazine in the tire, truck, and passenger-car fields carried a full-page "Open Letter To The Tire Trade."

The advertisements began: "Effective March 20, 1924, General will take on no new distributors for a period of three months. The object of this policy is to take the best possible care of our established trade."

Several long paragraphs followed which detailed General's successful sales record in the year just concluded, making the point "We could redouble our production facilities and take on additional distributors as an easier and quicker means of reaching this year's goal of 'More General Cords sold through dealers than any other make.' But we prefer to reach the goal by having fewer distributors do a bigger volume of business."

Buried in the long text was an especially telling paragraph: "Years ago it was freely predicted that when our time arrived we would yield to the temptation of selling every dealer willing to order a few tires. We don't want the 20,000 or 30,000 dealers our several competitors have. Last year, selling through just 600 distributors, General stood fourth in the industry."

The announcement concluded: "By June we expect to be in position to consider some new distributors. Meanwhile, our salesmen will devote their entire time and attention to established General distributors."

The ad was a sensation in the tire industry. No other tire manufacturer had ever turned down dealers. In fact, competitive salesmen fought strenuously to sign every conceivable dealer prospect in their territories. And, of course, the dealer-relations impact of the message was enormous: General Tire dealers became more sold on both the product and the policies of the company. Competitive dealers were envious as they read the announcement with dollar signs in their eyes. Many, including some of the largest metropolitan dealers in the country, could not believe that the ban on new dealers would be enforced, and applied for immediate franchises. All were required to stand in line until June 1, and all of them that General really wanted did so.

It was a remarkably successful campaign and, while based on the kind of "reverse pitch" W.O. loved, it nevertheless did have a firm factual basis in the record of the company: its fast growth, relatively small production capacity, and the necessity for adherence to high quality standards. But what many eager dealers read into the announcement was that General's 600 dealers did about as much business as competition's 20,000 or 30,000. That was a lot of business, a lot of profit.

Later, when the solicitation of dealers was resumed, W.O. coined the line "Quit carrying water for the elephants," the meaning of which was clear to the dealers for the big rubber companies with lines priced within pennies of each other, providing only a small dealer profit and heavy competition from identical tires on sale all over town.

One reason General's profits topped the million-dollar mark in 1923 was the fact that W.O.'s merchandising policies and methods were gaining momentum. The idea of buying a better tire that cost a little more was catching on, with the help of intelligent, dedicated dealers who made a good living from success in their communities. These dealers were not run-of-mine tire-shop operators, subsisting on submarginal profits. These were substantial, independent businessmen with exclusive franchised territories to develop as their own ingenuity and enterprise directed. Generally they belonged to the better clubs, participated in civic affairs, and were prominent in the business life of their communities.

As truck transportation became important, the dealers broadened their contacts into the trucking community, particularly because W.O. was an early enthusiast for truck transportation. As soon as the General passenger-car tire was established, truck tires with special advantages for various types of truck service were developed. For instance, General was the first to bring out an extra-heavy-tread tire for delivery trucks, the first to develop "drum-built" truck tires. Most important in establishing a close rapport with the trucking industry and a contribution to its development was General's pioneering and perfecting of recapping, a service obviously more important to truck operators than to passenger-car owners. A high-quality, factory-controlled system of recapping in many cases is the difference between profitable and losing trucking operation. Huge off-the-road tires, for instance, may cost several thousand dollars each, and under certain conditions may be put out of service by a rock cut after a few hours of operation. As it was for all big-size tires, the Kraft System was the first successful method of renovating them.

W.O.'s son Tom recalls an amusing incident in his father's office with Bill Coughlin, the Indianapolis dealer W.O. took on nocturnal prowls around the factory and had shown the original Kraft System experiment layout. Years later, Coughlin was having trouble with an "improvement" in the Kraft System. He was pouring out his troubles to W.O., who was busy about other matters. In a desperate effort to get W.O.'s attention, Coughlin positioned himself eyeball-to-eyeball with W.O. and asked, according to Tom, "Tell me, W.O., don't you think Herman Kraft is fifty per cent b.s.?" "About sixty per cent," W.O. shot back and went on working. It completely disarmed Coughlin and, somehow, conveyed the unmistakable conviction that Herman's remaining forty per cent was pure gold. W.O. would settle for human ore of that assay anytime.

As Tom's story suggests, the Kraft System was difficult to perfect and operate smoothly in the field. If it had not been, every tire company would have had it, or a system just as good. This is not quite true, either, because part of the success of the Kraft System had been due to the unique kind of dealer organization General had, and W.O.'s prime policy of having the factory work closely with each one.

"Change-Over to Generals." This widely advertised admonition was a key feature of W.O.'s merchandising strategy almost from the beginning. The germ of the idea came from the dress-pattern salesman who had called on W.O. in 1907 during O'Neil's brief period in his father's department store. The pattern deal included a generous trade-in allowance for competitive stock in an exclusive changeover to the new system.

The "cost more—worth more" tires were ideally suited to similar promotion. The plan required much dealer training, but was a success from the start. By the mid-1920s many prosperous new-car buyers all over America had already made a tradition of exchanging their brand-new tires for Generals. The dealer could afford to give a generous trade-in allowance for the original-equipment tires. He could resell them, and there was a substantial price difference for the Generals.

The success of General's changeover plan—both its profitability and its acceptance—annoyed the equipment-tire manufacturers in Akron more than any other General sales tactic. All of them introduced "premium" tires into their lines, but none made a comparable impact on the quality market. There were several reasons for this. General was established in the public's mind as exclusively a quality tire manufacturer. General's dealers knew how to sell the safety features of a quality tire, especially at the attractive price the changeover permitted. Equipment-tire dealers had no exclusive territory and competed against others handling the same line; hence they could not afford to carry the slow-selling premium tires in stock. A complete inventory presented a serious financial problem to these dealers. They were expected to stock at least four grades of tires in all the necessary sizes. This figure was almost doubled because most grades and sizes came in white and black sidewalls. Volume sales, not concentration of premium lines, were necessary to justify such inventories.

The Saturday Evening Post, which then conducted an annual poll of tire buyers' preferences, asked a standard question each year: "Regardless of price, which do you think is the best tire?" General scored the highest year after year, a remarkable tribute to General's quality reputation, because it made no original-equipment tires then. Persons responding to the questionnaire who were owners were fewer than those who were riding on the tires that came on their cars. They knew Generals only by reputation. It was a great tribute.

The changeover plan, then, annoyed General's competition in Akron. Car manufacturers also were disturbed by the widely advertised plan. The implication was that original-equipment tires were inferior, especially in the matter of safety.

Not until many years later, however, did the frosty atmosphere in Detroit become a problem. Then General's production capacity—greatly expanded with plants in Akron, Ohio; Waco, Texas; and Mayfield, Kentucky—was such that original-equipment tire business was desirable. General also had expanded into plastics, and the interior of almost every car—such items as roof liners, door panels, and upholstery—became a tremendous market for General's vinyl fabrics and foam rubbers. The diversification into metal products also made every automobile produced in America a potential user of scores of different kinds of metal component parts made by General.

Not until M. G. "Jerry" O'Neil—W.O.'s youngest son—became president in 1960 did the Detroit market really develop for General in a big way. The car industry's purchases of General tires, vinyl plastics, metal parts, and urethane foam were a big factor in producing General's first billion-dollar sales year in 1963, a record continued in 1964.

*The first national advertisement for
The General Tire appeared in* The Saturday
Evening Post, *January 27, 1917.*

What no tire-maker has ever done before

We've established throughout the United States, in a year's time, a tire success from every standpoint of performance, popularity and sales — established it with distributor, dealer and user. The General Tire stands out as the tire that stands up.

**A doubly
protective guarantee**

*The service must be 5000
miles or more — never less.
The actual mileage is
greater than the guarantee.
The General distributors
and dealers are anxious to
protect your interests, because our liberal guarantee
protects theirs.*

And we've done what no tire-maker has ever done before, because we did in the first place what no tire-maker *had* ever done before.

When we started, we knew what tire users wanted and needed — we knew how to make that kind of tire and we had the *will* to make it.

We had no old methods of our own to cling to through sentiment, stubbornness or economy. We had no old machinery or equipment that we had to get along with.

We had no past of our own to handicap us and we did have the pasts and presents of others to warn us of pitfalls in tire making.

In Akron we built a factory equipped with the very last word in tire making and perfecting machinery.

As you know, Akron is the center of the tire brains of the world. We located the best of the tire brains of

Akron and the world and put them to work in carrying out our ideals.

When you put to work the knowledge of a need — the know-how to fulfill that need — the machinery, equipment and materials to produce the results demanded by the know-how — the brains to see that results are produced, and the *will* to make a good tire, you can't make anything but a good tire.

There's the whole reason for the success of The General Tire — unvarying quality produced by building into it the best of Akron and the best of ourselves.

Now — after reading this, you are expecting the General to be a high-priced tire. Just ask the dealer and be surprised at how moderate the price is. And as to cost in service — the General costs less per guaranteed mile.

Write "General Tires" in your auto note book.

The General Tire & Rubber Company
Akron,   Ohio

THE *GENERAL* TIRE

BUILT IN AKRON

*Michael O'Neil, pioneer
merchant and founder of
the O'Neil clan in Akron.*

*First picture of the Akron General Tire group. It was
taken at the main entrance of the headquarters office
building around 1918. The "original five" are identified
by circles; First row (left to right): W. O'Neil;
Win Fouse; second row: Harold Pushee; last row
(left to right): Charlie Jahant; Bob Iredell.*

TOP: *The modern 14-inch automobile wheel was pioneered by General in the 1930's for use with the "Jumbo" tire which used only twelve pounds of air pressure. The Jumbo was sensational in performance, but was made obsolete after a year by wraparound fenders. W.O. is shown here with Frank Maranville, who with his son, A.G., originally designed the Jumbo as an airplane tire.*

BOTTOM: *Picture taken in 1925 showing General cord tire, one of the early truck tires of the company.*

W.O.'s enthusiasm for aviation caused General Tire
to have a fleet of eight company planes for business
use many years before this practice became common.
The 1928 photo (left) shows Bill O'Neil boarding one of
the "Sky Fleet" planes, taking off for a sales meeting.

*W.O. loved to walk through
the Akron plant. Not to
check on things, but simply
because his heart was tuned to
the pulse of the activity.*

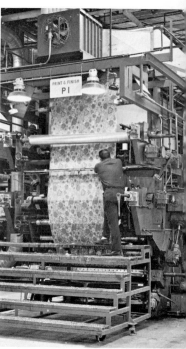

TOP LEFT: *General Tire is a major producer of Polyurethane foam.*

BOTTOM LEFT: *General Tire is the world's largest producer of vinyl-supported fabrics for automotive, furniture, and clothing industries.*

BELOW: *A giant rubber mill in operation, illustrating an important phase of tire manufacturing.*

A 1955 Business Week *photo of the O'Neils in a studio of WOR-TV. Left to right: Tom, John, Jerry, and their father.*

9

"Teach the boys about business"

O'NEIL'S FIRST million-dollar year; the success of his "no more dealers" campaign of advertising in the industry trade journals, which resulted in adding many important dealerships in metropolitan markets after the closed season ended; and the growing importance of the truck-tire market—many solid-tire truck fleets were being changed over to pneumatics—all combined to convince W.O. that he needed more executive manpower. But he loathed top-heavy organizations and private offices. There were only five private offices at General.

Over the years, the high mortality rate of rubber companies in Akron caused W.O. to comment that many of them "suffered as much from too many private offices as from too few sales."

W.O.'s greatest enjoyment was his work with the dealers. Scarcely an hour passed in which a franchise holder did not telephone O'Neil about some real or imagined problem, or the details of a prospective big commercial order. Some of the latter concerned truck-fleet changeovers or contracts with city cab or bus companies, some of which had already begun to prefer General tires because of their long, economical mileage and the interested service provided by the local dealer. After all, they were in his "exclusive territory," and he had a mother hen's concern for them.

Some long-distance calls also were from dealers who just wanted "to talk to the boss." It was a rare business day when one or two of the dealers—good personal friends—did not visit the factory. None of them would leave without dropping in on W.O. for a chat. (A chat with W.O. consumed about as much time as eighteen holes of golf does now.) O'Neil usually did most of the talking. The visitor gained more fun and profit listening to W.O. than he could have from interrupting the cascade of ideas.

As President, W.O.'s father Michael occupied a small private office when he was at the company. Those dealers who knew him paid courtesy calls on him. He was intelligent, kindly and gracious, but not a conversationalist. Bill Coughlin, the longtime Indianapolis dealer, always called on Michael when he visited the factory in Akron. Michael always greeted him with three questions, in this order: "How's your health? How's your business? Are you making any money?"

The latter two questions might seem redundant, but not to Michael. Doing a lot of business was not the same thing as making money. Charles Kellstadt, who retired as Chairman of the Board of Sears, Roebuck in 1962, managed a retail store in Akron when he was twenty-five. He knew Michael when the M. O'Neil Company was the largest store in town, and often ate lunch with Michael to pick up merchandising ideas. Years later, as Board Chairman of Sears, Kellstadt recalled that at one of these lunches Michael asked what was the most important item in a

merchandising budget—"What do you put down first?"
he asked. The young merchant who was to become head
of the largest merchandising operation in the world fum-
bled for an answer—fixed costs, cost of merchandise, some
other factors. The older man shook his head. "Young man,"
he said, "you don't know the first thing about running a
business. Ten per cent profit is the most important thing,
and that's what you put down first in making up a budget."
Kellstadt said he never forgot the advice.

Michael knew little about the tire business, and admit-
tedly was not greatly interested in it. Certainly he lacked
the passionate devotion to improve tires that infused
W.O.'s time and energies. But Michael was extremely
keen. He had a way of applying axioms of good general
business practices in a way which sometimes mystified the
men at General Tire who took a more specific view of the
day-to-day problems.

Bill Cahill, General's able first office manager and assistant secretary, was a practical man, as good office managers are likely to be. One day Bill (another of W.O.'s
classmates at Holy Cross) entered W.O.'s office with the
troubled appearance of a man who had just been through
an experience he could not understand. "W.O., your father
puzzles me. He just asked me again if we are paying our
bills on time and if we are taking our discounts. This is
all he ever asks me. He never asks whether our customers
are paying us, whether our costs are going up, what our
sales are. Nothing else. Just whether we are paying our
bills on time and whether we are taking our discounts."

W.O. chuckled long and often over that one. He knew
the trust his father placed in broad, basic business principles. In this case, Michael knew that if bills were being
paid on time so that the discounts could be taken, the
money was coming in. Michael relied more on this simple

fact than on sales totals or any other factor that could be answered simply.

Michael was conservative in business, but he never worried about borrowing money up to the total of the good accounts receivable. This was another of his basic business maxims which one does not hear expressed very often quite so simply and succinctly today. One wonders where Michael—"the quiet man," not gifted as was W.O. with a forcible, attractive sales personality—learned these rules of the game. He had a limited education, having left school to go to work at sixteen. There is no record or family tradition that anyone especially advised him. Was it all instinct? Did he read? And, if he did, who wrote the book that sparked the American dream in him?

W.O. admired his father tremendously. As a manufacturer who dared to be different—in an industry which looked upon product difference as heresy; faced with the necessity for constantly improving his product so that it would have a "worth more" difference, and helping his dealers to sell it at a "cost-more" price—these were problems Michael never had to face. Michael had others, but different ones.

From conversations at home as a boy and young man, W.O. learned from his father the principles of business. He would not have been equipped to take on, at twenty-three—even with the older Win Fouse as a partner—what was probably the largest tire-dealer territory of its time, had he not been acclimated to business by almost daily association with his father.

W.O. recognized this. As a young father of sons, he told a close associate many years ago, "I learned about business from hearing my father talk about it at home. I would like my sons to do the same thing. I don't intend to bore them to death, but I plan to talk a good deal about business and General Tires at the dinner table, evenings, and when we are together on vacations. I think it is up to me to carry on the family tradition and do what my father did: teach them about business while they are young."

Is there any explanation in heredity for the success of all the sons, without exception? It is all well enough to say that they were born to wealth and opportunity, but this does not explain their persistent ambition. There is a saying among the Irish that "every large family can afford one gentleman." And everyone knows that money has ruined as many young men as it has improved. Many large families of wealth have what the English call "remittance men"—sons who live at leisure in distant parts of the Empire on funds sent them by the family. And this country has had its share of their counterparts.

So, as a matter of interest in passing, all five sons of Bill and Grace O'Neil have distinguished themselves. To know them is to see the traits of W.O. and Grace combined in them: the down-to-earth philosophy of W.O., with an occasional vision thrown in, and the idealism of their mother. A sociologist probably would find deeper roots, but a layman's mind turns to the dinner-table conversation between Grace and W.O. with the children listening in. Here, one suspects, a tremendous amount of the family's solidarity was generated. The sons have said that their first interest in business came from these family conversations, and they credit their mother for giving ambition a spiritual quality by emphasizing, over and over, that wasted talents make a wasted life.

In 1925 and 1926, W.O. was faced with the first serious threat of "Washington interference" in what he regarded strictly an industry problem to be worked out by private enterprise, without government intervention.

Herbert Hoover, then Secretary of Commerce, was expanding the Department and its "services" to business. He invited leaders of industry to Washington to work with the government on the solution to their problems. Most executives responded with alacrity; a business story with a Washington dateline was always good for national release, and the "spokesman" for an industry could always depend on being widely quoted by the press.

Industry associations with Washington headquarters were established, including the Rubber Institute, of which W.O. was named a director. The Institute's first head was General Lincoln C. Andrews. Of him W.O. said at the time, "I like General Andrews personally, but he knows as much about business as any man who has been in the Army for thirty years." A retired military figure or other Washington personality was usually chosen to head these associations. Perhaps the best-known early example was Will Hays, President Harding's Postmaster General, who later became czar of the movie industry.

O'Neil did not like this trend. In his opinion the Department of Commerce was being used for propaganda. W.O. saw little difference between a government-business relationship by invitation and one by legislation. The result in any case was a misalliance, he felt, regardless of who did the wooing or whether it was a shotgun wedding.

Late in 1925, the crude-rubber price situation became quite complicated. Major tire companies, with Harvey Firestone as chief spokesman, persuaded Mr. Hoover that a government-sponsored campaign was needed to conserve rubber and help reduce the price of crude. Along with this campaign was the collateral objective of selling people the equally patriotic notion that they should buy tires made from reclaimed rubber.

In W.O.'s view, only a handful of English "short interests" and certain tire companies with rubber plantations could profit at that particular time from using less rubber to make tires. Inventories for 1926 tires had been bought at the high prices. Furthermore, economic forces were already at work to force down prices for the next year's inventory.

At any rate, Mr. Hoover was sold the necessity for a rubber-conservation program in late 1925, after W.O.'s commitments were made for his 1926 rubber purchases.

The government sponsored a huge "Rubber Conservation" program, assisted by the Rubber Institute's $500,000 advertising campaign and advertising sponsored by individual major companies. The use of reclaimed rubber became patriotic, and companies which advertised tires made from it were lauded.

There is no question that Bill O'Neil might have earned more money by conserving his high-priced natural rubber and substituting reclaimed stocks, as did all the others. But reclaim does not give good mileage and makes a weaker tire. To use it, W.O. felt, would ruin General's quality reputation. On April 10, 1926, he took a full page in *The Saturday Evening Post* for a personally signed statement under the headline: "Using Less Rubber Means Getting Back to Pre-War Mileage."

Part of his statement follows. To keep it in historic perspective, the reader should keep in mind that being against "Rubber Conservation" then was like coming out against the blood bank today:

> *You can't save rubber by using less of it.* The substitution of cheaper compounds for one-third of the pure rubber reduces the cost several dollars but, by weakening the entire structure, takes out two-thirds of the wear.
>
> Everyone knows what happens when cement is saved by the use of more sand in the batch. The principle is the same

whether it is tires or towers that totter. The way to save rubber is to make tires wear longer by using enough of it.

A boldface line at the bottom of the page read: "It's the second 10,000 miles that makes the big hit."

It was a source of great satisfaction to W.O. that a Firestone executive had two flat tires on his way to the office the morning the *Post* came out. His tires were of the new reclaimed rubber variety, of course, but W.O. said that "this was a coincidence."

The rubber market finally broke, enriching the London speculators as W.O. had predicted, and the rubber industry returned to work with, for a time, less Washington "cooperation"—a condition which was not to last for many years.

But after W.O.'s *Saturday Evening Post* ad appeared, he still had his high-priced all-natural rubber tires on hand and his dealers faced ruinous competition from the extremely low-priced reclaimed rubber tires. In this situation W.O. invented one of his most effective and longest-lived merchandising ideas—"The Trade-In Sale." Hammering constantly on the theme that Generals contained "not one ounce of reclaimed rubber," dealers advertised that they would "buy the unused mileage" in reclaim tires for safe, long-mileage Generals.

From the standpoint of moving tires in volume, the trade-in sale was a huge success. Many dealers sold out their entire stocks. There was actually a shortage of General tires before the year ended. But the trade-in value of the reclaim tires was low and cut company profits that year.

The trade-in sale was another W.O. innovation which annoyed competition, but the dealers learned how to use it effectively and profitably, so W.O. retained it. At first it was an annual event; now most dealers use it routinely throughout the year. Competitive companies have also adopted it, but less successfully.

Basically, the trade-in sale would seem a conventional enough merchandising idea. But it had never been applied to the tire industry before W.O. used it as a fiery example of his independence and militancy toward policies with which he disagreed.

In 1928 W.O. found a man to occupy the fifth or sixth private office at General. He "knew tires"—a special phrase in Akron that tells a lot about a man—and most of all he understood the "General Tire philosophy."

He was Loren Angus McQueen, a sales and advertising executive with B. F. Goodrich. It was uncanny how the Irish saints always sent W.O. the right man at the right time. There was the Bavarian Fouse, the Frenchman Jahant, the German Oberwinder, and now the Scotsman "Larry" McQueen.

A native of Superior, Wisconsin, and an alumnus of the University of Wisconsin, McQueen was one of the first of the new breed of college-trained sales administrators. He modernized and made more "scientific" General's sales machinery. He was also a great personal salesman. Until his time General had been in the replacement tire field exclusively. It had sold no tires to car or truck manufacturers for original equipment.

McQueen broke this barrier. In 1934 he persuaded the International Harvester Company to put Generals on its list of approved optional truck tires. W.O. agreed to the contract with considerable reluctance. He did not want to become a manufacturer of original-equipment tires, but finally acceded "because it was trucks."

Within two or three years, McQueen brought all truck manufacturers under similar contracts. The resulting volume became important to the company. It also helped—at just the right time in highway transportation history—to establish General Tire in the truck market. Truck owners, like passenger-car owners, tend to have their tires serviced through the dealer for the make of tire that comes on the vehicle originally, and also to replace with that make when the time comes.

The truck-tire volume from manufacturers' sales enabled General to pour more money into truck-tire research than otherwise might have been the company's inclination. Truck-tire-design innovations resulted which, by evolution and continued research, have made General a leader in the truck-tire field ever since. An entirely new method of manufacturing truck tires, known as "the drum method," was evolved, as will be described later.

Also, much later in McQueen's career—after World War II, in fact, and also after synthetic rubber and rayon had established themselves—he broke into the passenger-tire equipment field, negotiating large original-equipment contracts with both General Motors and Ford. In view of the traditional coolness between "Detroit" and General—chiefly because of General's changeover activities—the sale of original tires to car manufacturers was a notable feat of personal salesmanship. It was important to General because its production facilities had expanded so much that replacement business could no longer supply the tremendous volume of which General was capable. The idea that W.O. had dreamed in Kansas City had outgrown itself.

Shortly after joining General in 1928, McQueen began to take over the direction of the advertising which until then W.O. had supervised with a highly individualistic, instinctive feeling of what was "right" for General Tire. Under McQueen, General's advertising continued W.O.'s policies, particularly in projecting the quality image W.O. had envisioned as a necessity from the start.

Full-color pages and two-page spreads in national magazines repeated the prestige story. Newspaper advertising was used, principally on a cooperative basis with dealers, to promote local sales events and later such special items as the Winter-Cleat tire, the industry's first snow tire for passenger cars, when it was introduced as the General "2-in-1." This tire was one of W.O.'s most ingenious product ideas. It did not survive in the form W.O. had conceived, but it forced all tire manufacturers eventually to make a "snow tire" essentially the same as W.O.'s concept.

The "2-in-1" had a cleated tread, similar to that of all snow tires today. Dealers recommended that owners bring these winter tires to the shop in the spring to have the cleats buffed off, for quieter running after the snow season had passed. It did not take long to discover that most people's ingrained ideas about tire mileage made them reluctant to have any rubber buffed off their tires. As a result, the tread of the "2-in-1" was redesigned to provide good traction in snow and reasonably quiet running on dry pavement. In this form, the Winter-Cleat has persisted. Its sales have increased every year, and all manufacturers have a version of it in their lines.

Snow tires have become a necessity in many parts of the country, but they are basically a convenience specialty, and General Tire dealers are the most successful in selling them. Just as the "Change-Over to General" theme was countered by other manufacturers with premium lines, so was the Winter-Cleat specialty, but never with quite the same success. General Tire dealers rarely have enough Winter-Cleats to meet demand. Their success is another justification of W.O.'s insistence that dealers be creative merchandisers, knowledgeable about tires and interested in them as basic to safe, convenient motoring, not in just how many miles, with good fortune, they will run.

At one early point in Larry McQueen's handling of the advertising, W.O. developed tremendous enthusiasm for "bottling up towns." He had just driven from Florida—a rare event because the company had its own plane or planes from the late 1920s. On the trip, W.O. noticed that if General Tire had billboards at the city limits on the main highway on the edge of town in both directions, most drivers would see them. He also believed that such posters would be helpful in securing small-town dealers. Such a device W.O. called "bottling up towns." Complicated monthly posting schedules were worked out. The cost was not great—about $20,000—and for a few years the program was quite successful. Every time one of his friends returned from Florida and told W.O. that he had seen one of his posters, O'Neil renewed his faith in the plan.

"Bottling up towns" grew; dealers in bigger cities desired similar displays. Eventually General Tire became one of the largest users of outdoor advertising in America. The expenditure grew from the original $20,000 to more than $1.5 million. For many years General sponsored the largest outdoor campaign in America with local imprints. The dealer's name was printed at the bottom of each poster in boxcar letters thirteen inches high—only wooden type was available in such a size. The big display of their names appealed to the dealers' pride. The campaign was sound and popular, and was discontinued only when freeways and interstate-highway routes changed traffic patterns and eliminated many prime locations.

General Tire still believes in outdoor advertising. Many of its dealers use illuminated spectaculars and painted bulletins. One of RKO General's subsidiary properties is the Pittsburgh Outdoor Advertising Company.

Larry McQueen's contributions to General Tire were of many different kinds. They went far beyond the fields of sales management and advertising as the company proliferated. W.O. could find only one real fault with McQueen: he played golf too well. "No man with a job has any right to play golf in the low eighties," W.O. once said of him.

McQueen's first title at General Tire was that of trade sales manager. In 1940, he was made vice-president and five years later he was elected to the board of directors, of which he was made Honorary Chairman in 1961. He was also made a member of the boards of Aerojet-General and the A. M. Byers Company, General's wrought-iron and steel-pipe subsidiary.

For all his individualism and penchant for making his own decisions, W.O. assembled his key people regularly for a discussion of all phases of the business. The Monday morning meeting in Harold Pushee's office became a company tradition, begun in the earliest days of the company, and W.O. attended it faithfully until late years.

Very early in the company's history it became customary to invite groups of dealers to Akron. At first these assemblages were small enough to meet in W.O.'s office. At one of these in the 1920s, Art Rude of Los Angeles (later to play such an important role in Aerojet), Bill Hazlett of Youngstown, Jim Campbell of Pittsburgh, Ben Heer of Terre Haute, Bill Coughlin of Indianapolis, Howard Bischoff of Cincinnati, and a few others argued at length for a new pricing policy which W.O. opposed. The issue was undecided that day. In adjourning, W.O. called the men Bolsheviks, invited them to dinner and to "vodka cocktails." The next morning, the dissidents entered the meeting wearing red neckties. W.O. opened the discussion with the usual twinkle in his eye and said, "I am sorry to see you fellows spending your money just to flaunt your colors. However, everyone knows that General Tire dealers make a lot of money, and you have to spend it for something. I am glad an Akron store profited from you."

That evening—after the issue had been decided in favor of the "Reds"—there was a dinner at the Akron City Club. The dealers continued to wear their red ties. W.O. learned that the ties had been charged to his personal account at the M. O'Neil Company.

Later, annual meetings of the dealers, five or six hundred of them from Maine to California, were conducted in Akron. No Moslem ever trekked to Mecca with more religious fervor. There was always something new to see, talk about, and have explained—a new passenger-car or truck tire and later such things as improvements in the Kraft System.

Until McQueen put the programs on a more scientific basis, making them short courses in dealer education, the annual meetings were informal affairs. One ended memorably with a gunshot and pandemonium.

It was customary to close the afternoon session with a question-and-answer period. The questions, supplied by the dealers, were drawn from a box. Frank Gable, a colorful tire engineer in the old days with a flair for talking to the dealers, led up to the finale with a detailed account of tire construction. Concluding it, Gable said, "Now we will try to answer some questions that have been put in the question box." Drawing out one, he read it, adding, "Will the person stupid enough to ask that question please stand up?" After a moment's pause, one of the dealers in the middle of the room arose. Gable glared at him, shouted, "You ought to be shot!" Reaching under a pile of papers on the podium next to him, Gable seized a .38-caliber revolver, aimed it point-blank at the standing dealer, and pulled the trigger. The bullet was blank, but the resounding bang was real enough. Gable's reputation for volatility took precedence for a moment over common sense in the minds of many in the room.

The resulting panic, while not of heroic proportions, helped convince W.O. that his annual dealer meetings should be more scientifically based. As a result McQueen, head of Sales, delegated the department heads to prepare worthwhile talks on all phases of dealer operation. He was himself a master at talking to the dealers. Interesting charts explained all the talks, from truck-tire recapping potential in everyone's market to a new kind of tire construction or the company's advertising program for the coming year. Usually there was a new "selling movie" exploiting the company's latest premium passenger-car tire. Prints of these were made available to the dealers to use to close local sales. These innovations introduced by McQueen created the Annual Dealer Conferences, which became models of modern merchandising seminars. At first these too were held annually in Akron, but as the organization grew they were regionalized and held in cities throughout the United States. W.O. attended most of them, along with the younger department heads from Akron. This was a man-killing job—covering by air more than twenty cities for two-day sessions in a little more than a month. W.O. never seemed to tire of these trips. He enjoyed mingling with the dealers. And he had one advantage over the other executives—he was exempt from following McQueen's strictly enforced script, day after day.

A summary of General Tire's net profits after taxes for the 1920s shows that they exceeded a million dollars in every year beginning with 1923, except 1926, when the

"Rubber Conservation" hassle erupted. W.O.'s stubborn refusal to use "one ounce of reclaimed rubber in General Tires" cost the company at least a million dollars in profit that year, perhaps closer to two million. But it was invaluable in preserving and extending General's reputation for quality. His solution to the inventory problems of his dealers—the trade-in sale—enabled all of them to stay in business. At some expense to the company, he cemented loyalties of dealers and customers.

This is how the years of the 1920s returned net profits after taxes:

1921	$ 172,609
1922	921,572
1923	1,014,180
1924	1,282,375
1925	1,861,597
1926	370,585
1927	2,013,137
1928	1,590,653
1929	1,536,758

IO

General's pivotal decade

THE DECADES had a way of opening ominously in Akron. Just as 1920 was a catastrophic year, so 1930 ushered in the Great Depression. General, like other companies, suffered a severe decline in earnings—particularly in 1931 when the drop in inventory value of natural rubber was written off. By 1933 sales had picked up a little; earnings recovered somewhat and General's growth continued.

Because of the extremely bad conditions in the first three years and the slow recovery in the next three, General lost almost exactly as much as it made after taxes—about three and a half million dollars—from 1930 to 1938.

But General Tire was not knocked out by its massive competition during the Depression. The soundness of its thesis was proved. From that standpoint, the 1930s must be regarded as General Tire's pivotal decade. These were the years of low-volume, low-profit business. Most consumers bought—when they had to buy tires at all—anything "round and black and cheap." Their receptivity to General's "cost more—worth more" philosophy was at lowest ebb.

Adding to W.O.'s worries was his concern over the New Deal. He felt he was engaged in battle. The war had been declared against private enterprise by F.D.R. and by what W.O. liked to call the "New Deal group of college-professor theorists who knew nothing about business and were trying to run it."

Since O'Neil distrusted the reaction of most businessmen to the New Deal, for the most part he fought his own war. He did not pull up the moat and try to live out a siege. Rather he took to the field and fought. He was articulate and vehement in his denunciation of the government's "meddling" in business, believing that business and government should work opposite sides of the street. Hence he objected strenuously to the mild program of cooperation with business which Herbert Hoover inaugurated as Secretary of Commerce in the 1920s, and even more strongly to the coercive methods of the New Deal. His remarks, arguments, and criticisms were always consistent with his philosophy. He never tempered them, whether he talked in the relative privacy of his own office or testified at Washington hearings. There is no question that he made political enemies during this period, and also after the war when the government, in his opinion, dragged its feet on the issue of turning over synthetic rubber plants to private ownership.

The fact that he did not make more political enemies is a tribute to his best attributes: his honesty, frankness, practical logic, humor, and general likableness. He resembled Will Rogers in his down-to-earth analysis of situations and in his ability to give a humorous twist to his opinions in a sentence or two. Many who disagreed with W.O.'s intransigent views on politics and economics respected his total lack of hypocrisy. He was admired as a man and valued as a friend.

Not the only aspect of the New Deal which W.O. opposed, but the one which caused him the most frustration because it brought "outsiders in," was the administration's labor policy. This cost General a six-week strike in 1934, on the issue of recognition of a plantwide A.F. of L. union. This work stoppage occurred a year before the passage of the National Labor Relations Act, which established the rights of workers to organize and required employers to accept collective bargaining as a ruling principle in industry. Passage of the act was preceded by several years of labor unrest in Akron during the Depression and especially after 1932, when Congress outlawed the use of injunctions in labor disputes.

The long, drawn-out labor unrest—which affected all the plants in Akron—was partly responsible for General's lowered profits in the 1930s. The effect on the balance sheet was not W.O.'s chief concern, however. Anyone who knew him will give him credit for that. He had a deep philosophical conviction that the new labor policies created a form of collectivism that was unethical in itself and incompatible with the personal-liberty goals of a democracy.

W.O.'s relations with his workers were unique—especially for the president of an Akron tire company. By the 1930s he no longer knew the majority of employees by their first names, but he knew a high percentage of them. Many of them had been attracted to General in the first place by W.O.'s informality and fairness. A well-known fact in Akron was that no one ever lost his job at the old M. O'Neil Co., and as time went on it became apparent that the same tradition was followed at General Tire.

All of this caused unusually cordial management-employee relations, but no one thought of them in such formal terms. General Tire was just "a good place to work."

"W.O. is a great guy" was often heard. Many of the management people and dealers were the college-educated sons of men in the factory. A great many of the workers owned their own homes.

This is no attempt to make conditions sound idyllic. There were hard, dirty jobs to be done in the mill room. Tire-building was an exacting craft. No one ever compared the scent of cooking rubber with that of Chanel No. 5, but the conditions were a part of making Akron the Rubber Capital of the World and everyone had pride in his part of it. Also, it provided a good living with security for the future.

Some time before the passage of the National Labor Relations Act, the labor situation in Akron changed completely. Plantwide unions were organized, first as independent company unions and later as affiliates of the A.F. of L. or the C.I.O. Then strikes and work stoppages began to hit the major Akron rubber companies, although none had more than local effect because major companies all had plants in other cities to which production could be shifted if the Akron plant were struck. The effect upon the total tire production of these companies was negligible.

W.O. began to worry—chiefly about two things. One was that the leaders of these new unions "are not our people." The top echelon, at least, was composed of imported professionals skilled in union dialectics and organizing. W.O. never liked to talk about General Tire's business with outsiders, even the members of the Rubber Institute in Washington.

That this attitude was a very real deterrent to his acceptance of unionism cannot be questioned. But of even more practical concern to W.O. was General's one-plant status as a manufacturing operation. Unlike the other rubber companies, General had no out-of-town factories to which production might be transferred. General was 100 per cent vulnerable to paralysis in the event of a strike.

W.O. was realistic enough to understand that his vulnerability made General a prime target. There were times when he almost convinced himself that his relationship with his men was such that this could not happen, but the tide of events was running against this view. At about this time, on the suggestion of Jack Reed (the same Jack Reed who later brought the Yankee Network to W.O.'s attention), he almost bought a small Akron radio station to use as a communications line to his workers and, especially, to their wives. A great salesman, he had unbounded belief in the power of the spoken word to sell a good product or a good idea. The idea may sound quixotic now, but it had unexpectedly profitable results, as we shall see in the chapter dealing with that field of General Tire diversification which mystifies people so much—radio and television.

In 1940 General suffered its most severe strike. The fact that the issue was delayed so long must be regarded as proof of General's basically good labor relations, because the one-plant vulnerability of the company was as well-known to the union as to management. Soaring production of automobiles and trucks, year by year in the late 1930s as the Depression receded, brought increased demands from car and truck manufacturers for tires. Union regulations regarding hours resulted in the addition of extra shifts. Akron's traditional labor force was augmented by a great many emigrants from what has become known as Appalachia. Most of them had traditions, ambitions, and objectives quite different from those of the old-line Akron rubber workers—who had latex veins and carbon black in their blood. The newcomers were accused of being interested only in a high daily wage rate so they might work the minimum days a week required to pay living expenses, taking the rest of the week off. Whether this is true will probably always be debatable, like all premises based on a generality, but it is true that tire production began to suffer from a phenomenally high absentee rate.

The General Tire strike began on April 8, 1940, and ended June 26 without change in prestrike conditions. Not a long strike, as such things go. W.O. never believed in labels—except on tires—and probably never thought of himself as a "paternalistic" employer, but he took satisfaction in his relationship with his workers. He would interrupt any business conference in his office to recount, and chuckle over, something that Mickey Gannon in the garage or John Krelikowski, the elevator man, had told him on the way in. Perhaps the best way to describe W.O. is as a fraternalistic employer.

At any rate, the strike turned out to be a bitter affair before it ended, although fortunately no one was injured in incidents at the gates. The strike depressed W.O. Never again did he feel quite the same easy, natural camaraderie with his workers. If they wanted everything in the future to be in black and white, so be it. But W.O. did not believe this was to their advantage.

The General Tire strike occurred ostensibly over difficulties in connection with installing a new technique for building large sizes of truck tires, a method known as the "drum process." It had been used in building passenger-car tires and the smaller sizes of truck tires for years. W.O. conceived the idea of conducting research to extend the process to the big sizes. The lower manufacturing cost might eke some profit from the post-Depression years. The process was a highly original way to relieve the profit squeeze which had developed as a result of the higher mileages first-line passenger-car tires delivered in comparison with the tires of the 1920s. Then the normal life expectancy of a tire had been about 3500 miles. By 1940 it was about 20,000 miles. Although passenger car and truck registrations had expanded tremendously in the interim, the increase in unit tire sales was nowhere so great. This restriction was particularly hard on General, which depended on the replacement tire market. W.O. saw that a method of substantially reducing the cost of truck-tire production, without affecting quality, would help solve General's problem and be a progressive step for the burgeoning truck industry.

Actually, General built the first truck tire by the drum method in 1934, after investing considerable money in research and the necessary new factory machines and equipment. As research and testing continued, the technique was extended successfully to larger and larger sizes until, in 1940, General began to build the largest highway-truck tires by this advanced method. The event was an important technological breakthrough, which the industry followed, a development which would be invaluable to the war effort a few years later. If W.O.'s drum method of building truck tires had not been adopted when it was, the essential volume of wartime military and civilian truck tires could not have been achieved or sustained. Tire-builders could be trained more quickly; production became 50 per cent faster; the product was more uniform; and unit cost was reduced.

When production of the highway-truck size of tire by the drum method was started in the General plant, the president of the union was a General employee working on truck-tire production. He demanded that he be paid for routine production of truck tires a piece rate as high as a competitor paid for experimental production of a single casing. When this was refused, he walked out, persuading others to leave with him. The walkout occurred on April 8, although no strike vote was taken until two days later. The plant remained open during the dispute. The foremen and others who reported for work continued to make tires, but total production for April, May, and June was approximately 70 per cent below normal. The curtailment devastatingly affected General's inventory of tires for the remainder of the year. Many of the most popular sizes—passenger-car and truck—were completely out of stock for months.

Nineteen forty must have been O'Neil's most frustrating year in business. Before the strike the first jolt was a completely unexpected price cut by Goodyear. The industry followed suit. W.O. thought the Goodyear reduction was triggered by a belief that the mail-order houses and oil companies, featuring low-price tires, were encroaching on its market.

O'Neil confirmed this explanation by a shift in emphasis which Goodyear initiated with its price cuts from first-line to lower-line tires, a policy which the other three largest-volume tire companies joined. W.O., the great exponent of human mileage, especially for the family man and for "those who would be missed in the community," was particularly distressed that Goodyear's advertising campaign featured a statement by the president of the company that he personally used a Goodyear tire recognized as second-line by the trade. As a quality-tire manufacturer committed to a "costs more—worth more" policy, W.O.'s sales philosophy was built on raising people's sights about tires. General could not accept the unexpected trend, and sales suffered.

This bit of industry lore had an interesting prologue.

Goodyear, many years before, was the first major rubber company to make tires for Sears, Roebuck. This alliance motivated Harvey Firestone's decision to sell a wide variety of hardware items—especially appliances—in Firestone tire stores. Firestone was determined to profit as much from Sears-type merchandise as Sears did from the Goodyear-built tires. W.O. persuaded his dealers to stay out of the "hardware business."

"You can make more money out of selling General tires," he said, "than sitting in the office talking to toaster salesmen."

It will be remembered that O'Neil's first tire-selling experience in the southwestern territory had convinced him that hardware stores did not make the best tire outlets. He had proved that even the smallest operation requires somebody's full attention. A large shop required an organization under the constant direction of someone with the dedication of a priest, the shrewdness of a lawyer, and the concern of a physician for people's physical well-being.

There is, however, a tangential comparison. While Harvey Firestone expanded into the business of selling miscellany to recoup sales profits, there is evidence that W.O. was influenced to enter radio "to make as much out of advertising as it is costing us." How serious he was about this as a major motive may be questioned, but he made the comment once or twice, so the possibility occurred to him. And this course seemed more sensible to him than expecting his tire dealers to compete with Sears.

The General Tire strike in 1940, along with the industry's emphasis on low-priced second-line tires, combined to make the year a very disappointing one for General Tire. Profits dropped to $595,917. The year before they had bounded to an all-time high of $2,137,318 after taxes, an encouraging performance after the lean, profitless, or losing years of the early and mid-1930s. W.O. always believed that 1940 would have been General's first three-million-dollar-profit year except for the strike and the industry's irrational interest in cheap grades of tires.

W.O. once said that the Depression made him decide to diversify. In that case, the Depression was obviously the most fortunate event in General Tire history. Despite the Depression and the resultant loss of tire business, W.O. plunged ahead.

He led his company into more concentrated research and development of new tire ideas during the decade of the 1930s than did any other tire company. He had to. Improved ideas were the lifeblood of his company. They gave his tires a salable difference over conventional, lower-priced tires. His "cost more—worth more" equation was still effective, but a lot of "worth more" was required to make just a little "cost more" palatable during the Depression times. A higher-priced product always has to be of better quality to keep customers coming back; the General Tire dealer depended on repeat sales.

Other activities blossomed. In the 1930s W.O. blazed the way to today's truck tire by pioneering the method which cost him the 1940 strike, but which was so logical that it could not be stopped and was universally adopted by the industry.

In the 1930s, too, a tremendous amount of research, development, and testing time and money were invested in the Kraft System. The nation's only factory-controlled system of tire recapping was so useful to truck owners by the late 1930s that they could not imagine how they had operated without it. A few years later, during the war, they could not have.

Also in the 1930s—twenty-five years ahead of the industry—W.O. achieved his Kansas City dream of a unique tire design that took fullest advantage of rubber's resilience, used very little air pressure, and yet gave good mileage and was easy to steer. Such a casing was developed by a father-and-son team at General, Frank and A. G. Maranville. Their discovery was not an automobile tire at all, but one ideally suited for airplanes, and was so patented. At that time, the landing gear of planes was not retractable and conventional "doughnut" airplane tires set up tremendous wind resistance. General's new product, known as the Streamlined Smooth Contour Tire, was like adding horsepower to an airplane's engines by reduction of wind friction. Cruising speeds were tangibly improved. Takeoffs, especially in the slush of the not-so-well-maintained runways of the day, were improved. Landings were softer. The Streamlined Smooth Contour Tire seemed to have a bright future in aviation. Then, quite soon, due to no shortcomings in the performance of the tire, its career ended abruptly. The retractable landing gear was developed; the aerodynamically correct design of the SSC was not needed, and its shape did not fit the new tire nacelles.

Undaunted, W.O. decided to make the new invention into an automobile tire, although it bore little physical resemblance to tradition. It had an enormous air cavity, but a patented construction made the tread narrow, reducing rolling resistance and contributing to steering ease. It operated with only sixteen pounds of air. The effect on the ride sensation of the cars of the 1930s was phenomenal. As a publicity stunt, the mayors of almost every city in the United States were driven up and down the City Hall steps by local dealers. No one sued, so there must not have been any sacroiliac dislocations. Owners learned to their delight that they could drive across railroad tracks or along the ties, over curbs, and even on the county roads of the era without discomfort.

A few years earlier, "orthophonic sound" had been introduced and had swept the country. It was a radical improvement in the sound quality of phonograph records. One New York automotive editor saw the new General as the same kind of milestone in the field of automobile tires. For the new tires, W.O. sentimentally revived the name Jumbo, which had first been used ten years earlier on General's first oversize tire. The new Jumbo required special fourteen-inch wheels—twenty years ahead of their time. They were intended for light cars, such as Fords and Chevrolets, and a set of tires and wheels sold for about $250—a good down payment on the car in those Depression times.

To spur the interest of the sales organization of Scanlon-Lewis, then General Tire dealers at Rochester, Joe Grady (New York state manager and later Syracuse dealer) offered a bonus of $10 a set during the month of May, provided fifty or more sets of Jumbos were sold in Rochester. He had no authority to make such a deal, but thought he had set the quota high enough to be safe. Actually, sixty-eight sets of General Jumbos, at $250 a set, were sold by Scanlon-Lewis that May. Grady was criticized by "the factory" for making the unauthorized offer, but not too seriously. The tremendous sales accomplishment by the Rochester dealership soon was matched and exceeded throughout the country. The Jumbo, ruled out of the sky by a major change in plane construction, became a huge success on the ground.

But, again, not for long. Next year's cars had wraparound fenders. The Jumbo could not fit under them and soon went out of production.

Both the Streamlined Smooth Contour Airplane Tire

and the Jumbo were outstanding in performance. The Jumbo especially represented the realization of W.O.'s twenty-year dream. Many a man would have eaten his heart out in disappointment; the failure of many of a life has been blamed on less. But when continued production of the Jumbo became impractical, W.O. dropped it from the line with a shrug, and no one ever heard him voice any sentimental regrets. One of the lessons of O'Neil's life was that he had so many dreams and ideas that the failure of one or two was an incident, not a crisis.

It was also true that tire design was beginning to move in the direction of his thinking, and it would not be too many years before most of his ideas would become practicable.

The Jumbo's death anticipated one of General's longest-lived successes, a unique tread designed by Herman Kraft. This first appeared on the General Dual 10, later with modifications on the somewhat lower-priced Dual 8, and eventually on the General Squeegee.

The nomenclature is of some interest. The word *dual* has always been a favorite in General Tire's lexicon. It started with the Dual Balloon, introduced by General in the very early 1920s. There have been others, including the famous Dual 90, offered in the late 1950s, and improved and modified several times since. At any rate, *dual* is a General Tire word. It's short; it molds well on a tire, and no other tire manufacturer has picked it up.

After several years of outstanding sales success and customer satisfaction, General decided to modernize its names. The company was ready to introduce a new tire which incorporated basically the same tread, but with some new features deemed worthwhile. At just this time, the Federal Trade Commission issued a "cease and desist" order against the use of the names Dual 10 and Dual 8.

The FCC took the position that the names meant the Dual 10 had ten plies and the Dual 8 eight plies. By the same line of reasoning, General's modern Dual 90 would have had ninety plies.

It may be that because of the industry's peculiar advertising over the years, some people are unaware that a tire offering extra resilience and the utmost in riding comfort could not possibly have eight or ten plies. But it is more likely that most people would not know plies from a pair of pliers; or that, in fact, tires had them. If they did, all they had to do was go to a General Tire dealer and try to buy a General Dual 10 or Dual 8 where a salesman would have been delighted to "bore hell out of them" with the engineering explanation. There was even a ten-minute movie with animated diagrams. Few buyers got out without viewing it. Seeing the movie was a practically mandatory ritual before anyone was allowed to buy, because the film cost the dealer a hundred dollars.

But the government has its insistent ways. The names Dual 10 and Dual 8 were banished by the FCC. Their memory lives on in happier repute in the minds of veteran dealers, salesmen, and owners as the finest tires ever built up to that time.

The General Squeegee was named for its distinctive tread which, with improvements, carried over from the Dual 10 and Dual 8. This model was by all odds the simplest and most effective tire tread ever developed. The tread consisted of continuous circles of closely spaced rubber rings running circumferentially around the tread. There was no complex "nonskid" pattern cut into the tread; no buttons, knobs, or projecting ribs. The patentable idea of the tread was that the closely spaced rubber circles were deeper than they were wide. This resulted in the tread's "becoming alive," so to speak. The industry's first truly flexible tread, the novelty was sometimes referred to as "action traction." As long as the car was running, the continuous rubber rings of the tread provided a smooth, quiet ride. The moment the brakes were applied, however, the narrow, closely spaced rings tended to "wrinkle"— "flex into a serpentine pattern," in the words of the patent —and produce an unusually quick and straight-line stop. The performance was especially noteworthy on wet pavements. The flexible rubber rings tended to wipe dry the pavement when they went into action, like a window-washer's "squeegee." Hence the name, which was originated by a driver in General Tire's test fleet whose identity unfortunately is not known.

In General's Fiftieth Year the company's super-tire was the famous Dual 90. This was, of course, by that time a tubeless tire of which one feature was the viscous material on the inside which sealed punctures as it rolled. This was an accident-preventing feature on the highway and in traffic and was a great boon to women drivers, especially. The sealant was such that nails and other puncturing objects could be withdrawn later, with no air loss and no need of repair.

The puncture-sealing feature was undeniably important and was possible only after the tubeless tire had been perfected. Some years before, while tubes were still in general use, the industry had become infatuated with puncture-sealing tubes. General had one which was regarded as the best in the industry. At the annual meeting of dealers at the Hotel Roosevelt, in New York, the tube sales manager, an excellent speaker, spent a half-hour extolling the virtues of the General puncture-sealing tube. Everyone was impressed and, no doubt, determined to give more attention to a phase of the business on which he had not fully capitalized. W.O.'s closing remarks came next on the program. His opening sentence was: "I do not like puncture-sealing tubes; they ruin tires."

II

"Little fellows" and
the future of America

Bill o'neil was a conservative in politics, a Republican, an admirer and supporter of United States Senator Robert A. Taft. In the Senator's 1944 campaign for re-election, W.O. strongly urged the use of an outdoor-poster advertising campaign. In overseeing the layouts for the statewide billboards, W.O. discovered that BOB TAFT could be used in very large type on one line. He recommended strongly this form of the name instead of the more formal Robert A., which would necessitate smaller type. His recommendation was accepted. This billboard campaign marked the first time Ohio's Mr. Republican presented himself to the electorate by the informal Bob Taft.

The only Presidential campaign in which W.O. was involved personally was that of Wendell L. Willkie in 1940. This was largely the result of personal loyalty. Willkie had practiced law in Akron from 1914 to 1923. He had been W.O.'s lawyer and a director of a bank of which W.O. was the chairman. The two men were friends, especially during Willkie's Akron residence, and while they did not resemble one another facially, they were of the same physical type—big, broad-shouldered, rugged, quick of movement, good conversationalists, both given to expressive hand gestures. Swinging down the sidewalk in Akron, talking and gesticulating, they might easily have been mistaken for brothers.

At about the time of the Willkie Presidential campaign, W.O.'s interest in radio was increasing. He believed that a campaign of spot announcements might help Willkie carry Ohio. O'Neil even created the format, and it was a good one. The Campaign Committee approved a heavy schedule of radio throughout Ohio. Probably no political spots before or since had higher impact and remembrance value. Basically the format was simple. A bell rang, and an announcer's voice said: "Willkie rings the bell again!" Then came fifty seconds of trenchant Willkie comment on a principal campaign issue.

It was not learned until after the election that the bell unfortunately sounded to some people like a telephone bell. Many householders were in the yard; housewives were in the bath or in the basement doing laundry. After rushing to answer the phone, their receptivity to the Willkie message was low. The fault was one of production; and, as advertising-agency men say, you can't blame the creative department for a typographical error. W.O.'s idea should have received a better production follow-through. Willkie lost Ohio, but the experience did not weaken W.O.'s faith in radio. His interest in the medium extended beyond a schedule of political spot announcements.

W.O. could be unpredictable. He could be impulsive, and he could procrastinate. He could be orthodox, and he could be iconoclastic. All of which means, of course, that he had a complex personality in spite of his direct nature in face-to-face contacts with people. He was notably independent and individualistic. As one competitor said, "I wouldn't mind his being independent if he weren't so imaginative about new ways of showing it."

W.O. was, however, predictable in his position toward government participation in the affairs of business. Let us call it participation for the moment. After the New Deal days he called it "interference" or "meddling." But he was opposed to government in business, as we have seen, even in the form of a friendly handclasp from Secretary of Commerce Herbert Hoover. Government cooperation was little more palatable to him than government coercion. So on this subject he was consistent and predictable. He knew that politics made strange bedfellows, but felt that business was the strangest of all. "Politicians don't know anything about business and businessmen don't know anything about politics, so the two ought to stay completely apart." He thought the country would be better off if they did.

W.O. was a vigorous opponent of antitrust acts all his business life. He regarded them as unwarranted intrusions of government in business affairs. The fact that the parent of them all—the Sherman Anti-Trust Act—was enacted in 1890, a generation before he started in business in Kansas City, and was accepted by most businessmen as casually as the typewriter was of no consequence to him. The principle was wrong, he said, and he opposed it. His life-long position on this subject is interesting and revealing because he held it when he was a small manufacturer in an industry of giants. A lesser man in a similar competitive situation might have decided he had something to gain from the government's restraining of his big competitors. Not W.O.

"When the big tire companies got into a price war," he used to say, "tire prices never came down enough to benefit the public. In the hifalutin' language of the government people, no 'social good' came from it. On the other hand, the profits of dealers were seriously affected. No tire manufacturer was ever forced out of business by a price war, but thousands of dealers have been ruined over the years, some of them with investments of ten thousand dollars and even less. They have been forced to the wall by a senseless price war. To prevent such foolishness by allowing manufacturers to agree on a price below which they will not sell their tires would be a violation of the price-fixing provisions of the antitrust laws. This benefits no one; not the public, who would save but a few cents per tire. It victimizes thousands of small dealers. Even those it doesn't wipe out of business it forces into the red, and the ones it affects least are the big manufacturers."

Because W.O. began his career in the tire business as a dealer and made profitable local dealerships the keystone of General's sales policy, his views on this subject were expert, although he would have rejected that term. "An expert," he one said, "is never worth a damn as an executive. He knows too much and all he sees is problems."

W.O.'s son John remembers an entirely different facet of W.O.'s consistent—but losing—fight against government intrusion into business. In April 1948 Paul G. Hoffman, once president of the Studebaker Corporation, was named Economic Cooperation Administrator of the European Recovery Program, better known as the Marshall Plan. Soon after his appointment by President Truman, Hoffman outlined the aims of the program at a dinner in New York for leading industrialists.

After the affair, W.O. accompanied by his son John,

approached Hoffman. Hoffman detached himself from a conversational group to meet them.

In a few words, W.O. made clear his opposition to government-to-government aid. He pointed out that the benefits would be diluted by bureaucratic inefficiency, both here and in the nations receiving the aid. He said that unstable and unpopular governments would use the grants politically and defeat the program's purpose for the United States, both from a practical humanitarian point of view and as propaganda. More effective, W.O. told Hoffman, would be a policy to encourage American businessmen to sell abroad by using the lend-lease funds as guarantees against loss. In this way credit could be extended to the "little fellow" in foreign countries. Small farmers and businessmen abroad could be helped to build a progressively improved economy, as had been done in the United States since the days of the first farm machinery. This would provide the United States a world-wide testing ground for the private-enterprise system which has done so much for the "little fellow" in America. W.O. wanted a man-to-man—"people-to-people"—approach, not a government-to-government relationship with all its red tape and diplomatic complexities. This probably was the first "people-to-people" approach suggested to the government. Many years later, during the administrations of President Eisenhower, the phrase became popular, but the program was never implemented as W.O. had suggested.

Hoffman seemed abstracted during the conversation, and John thought he might have been giving the ideas serious consideration. Later John concluded that Hoffman knew that the issue had been decided. In view of the difficulties of the foreign aid program, as W.O. predicted, speculation is interesting on the possible effects of W.O.'s idea. At least private business would have been a political buffer. Industry, not "the flag," would have been blamed for offended political sensibilities. And, W.O. believed, there would not have been so many mistakes.

The Kansas City tire dealer had come a long way—now giving advice on international business affairs—but even in 1909 he had wanted "a whale of a territory." He had carved out a lot of it and had built a business soon to gross a billion dollars a year. Few men in the history of America have done that, and not to listen to any idea of his with a dollar sign in front of it—whether government or private money—was a mistake.

W.O. had a typically original theory regarding the origin of the American dream. He believed it began with the extension of credit to "the little fellow." And he pronounced *fellow*—which he used often, usually in the plural in talking to his associates and at dealer meetings—not in the precise diction of an Oxford don or as *fella*, but as something halfway between. The accent was a very warm, human way of talking to and about his fellow man.

W.O.'s suggestion to Paul Hoffman advocated putting into effect overseas the credit phenomenon which he always regarded as the beginning and the basis of the American dream in the industrial age. He believed that America became a great nation of resourceful individuals more universally adapted to the use of machines because they were more knowledgeable about mechanics than other peoples. This caused Americans to use more and more machines to create an ever-rising standard of living for themselves. What started their familiarity with machinery was the fact that the farm reaper and mower people, about 1880, started to sell their machines to the farmer— "the little fellow"—on credit.

Because they held notes for most of the purchase price, the manufacturers made sure that the machines worked.

[128]

They taught the farmers how to operate the equipment, and instructed dealers in each area to keep close watch on the machine's performance. Chronic trouble was reported to the factory and improvements were made in the next model. "If you wanted to know what was wrong with last year's reaper," W.O. said, "all you had to do was to read what improvements were being made this year."

The dealer's service man and the farmers in his area worked closely together. As the farmer's familiarity with the machine increased, he often made valuable suggestions for improvements, based on actual experience in the field. Very often these ideas showed up in the next model. The man with the hoe disappeared and the American farmer with a screwdriver and pliers in the back pocket of his overalls became the basic symbol of American mechanical know-how.

W.O. liked to point out that no other country has as many men familiar with mechanical devices as does this country. He had a number of stories to illustrate this. One favorite went this way: "My kid Tom, who was a beachmaster during the war in the South Pacific, told me that Japanese forces, abandoning captured American trucks and Jeeps in a hurry, knew of no better way to disable them than to throw dirt on the engine, which could be quickly hosed off. Any American high school boy would have known enough to take out the distributor caps or the spark plugs."

The necessity for the early mower and reaper people to provide service after the sale in order to make sure of collecting on the notes the farmer gave them for most of the purchase price set a pattern for manufacturer's service in the United States which is found nowhere else in the world, according to W.O.

If you buy an automobile in England, you get service

from a general garage, which repairs all makes of cars. Only in America does the car manufacturer provide after-sale service for each particular make of car. W.O. felt that this was a modern extension of the mower and reaper idea —extending credit to "the little fellow" and making sure the investment paid off. The factory dealer also shared a "pride of product" which a general garage does not have, and possessed greater knowledge of the machine, based on information constantly supplied him by the factory and frequent contacts with factory representatives.

W.O. argued that the ability of the American farmer to outproduce the peasants in other countries of the world was the result of his superior mechanical knowledge. This trait accounted for our natural inclination to accept new machines and to replace them with improved models. In this way we had adjusted to the industrial age better than other people and, consequently, had a higher standard of living. He was interested enough in the subject to assemble arresting conversational statistics about it. "America is the world's leading food producer because the American farmer produces an average of eight times as much food as his counterpart anywhere else," he said. He also pointed out that in the early days the surplus food produced by twenty farmers went to feed one city-dweller. Finally, twenty farmers could feed about sixty city-dwellers and ten living in other countries. Almost all of this agricultural progress W.O. attributed to farm machinery, the mechanical know-how of American farmers, and especially to the attentive service policies of their manufacturers. This kept existing machines operating well and produced frequent improvements.

W.O.'s belief in the importance of service to the customer caused him to emphasize the service end of the tire business much more than was generally done before he created the General exclusive-territory franchise. Until then, service in the tire business had been regarded as a necessary evil, confined mostly to the repair of flat tires.

General, of course, made truck tires almost from the very beginning. It leased bus tires on a mileage basis to many leading companies in cities, and passenger tires to taxicab companies because of General's high-mileage reputation. In the truck field, the Depression gave W.O. the opportunity to put into practice his "credit-for-the-little-fellow" credo. Most truck companies then were small, one-family or partnership businesses. The owners were hard-working, rugged individualists, and W.O. knew many of them. He admired all of them except the "price-cutters." The practice of cutting rates became prevalent during the Depression, before truck lines went under Interstate Commerce Commission tariff regulations, and some of W.O.'s best trucker friends were being seriously hurt by this competition.

One of the reasons General Tire enjoys a preferred position among many of the largest trucking companies today is that in the early 1930s W.O. extended credit to "little fellows" struggling against price-cutters. Credit for tires was extended and in some cases loans were granted for new trucks, repairs, payrolls, and fuel. All W.O. wanted to be sure of was that the man was honest, hard-working, and not a price-cutter. The companies of these "little fellows" are among those which have developed into today's highway transportation giants. The sons or early associates of the founders of these companies know the tradition that applies—the payroll that was met, the broken axle that was replaced, or the truck that came down off jacks when the General Tire dealer appeared one morning during the Depression and said "W.O. wants to help."

Most of the truck companies which have "gone public"

have done so in recent years. The trend began shortly before O'Neil's last illness. He heartily approved of it. In fact, he heartily approved of "Wall Street." Unlike Michael, W.O. felt that Wall Street offered the "little fellow" the means to participate in the ownership of American businesses. He thought the speculative aspect of the market was overplayed. He encouraged no one to speculate or, for that matter, to make short-term investments in stocks. But he felt that, just as in the agricultural age of this country, when a young man looked forward to owning a few acres of ground, people should in industrial times feel the same way about owning a few shares of stock in American industry. He felt that the widest possible distribution of shares was desirable from every standpoint, including the strengthening of America's private-enterprise system.

W.O. was disappointed to learn from a New York Stock Exchange survey made in 1952 that in a country of 175 million people there were only six and a half million individual shareowners of publicly held companies. He felt that the long-term capital-expansion requirements of industry would be enormous, particularly in view of the costly new technologies and the needs of our increasing population. "The private enterprise system is being built on too small a base. A whole lot more 'little fellows' are going to have to invest in the future."

W.O. had an experience in a European country which convinced him that the right in this country to buy stock in leading corporations amounts to a Fifth Freedom, although there is no case on record of a politician having advertised it as such. W.O. was calling on a European industrialist whose business was among the very largest in the country, with several highly profitable subsidiaries in other countries. The purpose of W.O.'s call was to express his gratification over how well General Tire's technical services had worked out in the manufacturer's tire plant over a period of about a year and, in a spirit of cordiality, W.O. mentioned that he would like to buy some stock in the business. His host's face took on a puzzled expression. "Why, Mr. O'Neil," he said, "you don't understand. There is no stock. I own this business."

W.O. was incredulous. He came away from the interview more convinced than ever that Americans do not fully appreciate the opportunities they have to participate in the ownership of corporations through investments in good stocks. It seems that nearly everyone had an uncle who lost all the family fortune in the Smathers Smokeless Lamp Wick Company, or some such, and all the twentieth-century corporations on which our economic future is based suffer as a result, at least insofar as public acceptance of their securities is concerned. At least this was W.O's conclusion.

W.O. never succumbed to the temptation of copying the advertising of his Akron competitors. Other manufacturers in Akron tended to imitate each other. If high mileage was the theme of one, then high mileage was likely to be the theme of all. Or it might be price. Many observers feel that this age-old practice in Akron of "advertising to one another" has had an unfortunate effect upon the public's ability to differentiate between tire brands. Tires have become faceless products, probably more so than any other consumer product backed by multimillion-dollar advertising campaigns. The leading popular magazines conduct surveys among car owners every year, and a startlingly high percentage do not even know the make of tire on their car. Those who have Generals know, and the quip among competitors in Akron is "they know because they cost more." Generals do cost more, but the advertising, the dealers, and the entire sales force sell the idea that "the least of the difference is the difference in price." Modern low-profile tires and wrap-around fenders obscure the tires on cars today, but W.O.'s original idea of a "cost more—worth more" tire sells to repeat customers year after year, so there must be more to the preference than the mere pursuit of vain prestige. W.O. believed there will always be opportunity in America for a distinctive product, backed by the power of a good selling idea—and good service.

12

"A whale of a territory" goes global

THE MAN who had wanted "a whale of a territory" when he began as a Kansas City dealer in 1908 with the whole Southwest to work on began to realize this phase of his dream on a global basis in 1933.

He was not interested in adding foreign subsidiaries as such. In addition to the expense, the risk would bring him into head-on competition with large British, European, and American companies who were already firmly entrenched. Furthermore, it was not a creative approach. The company was already doing a fair amount of export business, and W.O. felt that just building a factory here and there was not the answer.

It is important to keep in mind that this was 1933. The Depression would have deterred most companies from expanding, especially into the foreign field. At the same time, as early as 1930, the whole system of private enterprise and its ability to lead the country—to say nothing of the world—out of its economic doldrums had begun to be seriously questioned. W.O. passionately believed in private enterprise.

There is evidence that he began thinking about international operations as early as 1930. In that year he hired as export manager Joseph A. Andreoli, who had served in the same capacity at India Rubber, which General later bought and which, in 1930, was doing 60 per cent of its business in the export field.

In 1933, General had a branch in Mexico City, managed by C. A. Guijarro. A large part of its competition, not only in Mexico City but also throughout the country, came from a tire known as El Popo, which was made by a firm under Mexican ownership. El Popo was not a very good tire by General's standards, but it had a large share of the market because Mexicans were loyal to it.

El Popo's management was aware of General's better quality, too, and a small party of top officials came to Akron to explore U.S. tire-building operations. It would be unreasonable, they thought, for a direct competitor to tell them much, especially since they had no definite plan but merely wanted to discuss general practices. Someone in Akron, however, told them of W.O's easy approachability, so they decided to call on him. One reason for their original reluctance was that they had no definite plans to discuss; they merely wanted pointers on how to build a better tire.

As they talked, W.O. got an idea. Such was the birth of General's fresh and brilliantly successful approach to international markets, with emphasis on private-enterprise methods and the broadest possible base of ownership among the citizens of the many countries in which General Tire International affiliates have come to be located.

The new administration of President Abelardo Lujan Rodriguez was dedicated to a program of industrial expansion "by Mexicans." The participation of foreign investors and managers was not welcomed. Despite this, W.O. received an invitation from President Rodriguez to come to Mexico City to discuss his plan. The invitation came a few days after El Popo's men had returned. So W.O. flew down. He took no legal counsel or technical advisors with him.

Evidently the two men took to one another at first meeting. General had already been deluged with ideas about how the company should be run, and, at one point, W.O., with that crinkly-eyed smile that was his enigmatic trademark, said, "General Rodriguez, your people want to run El Popo as we run the United States. We want to run it as you run Mexico."

The remark made a great hit with the President. He laughed heartily, and laughed again when he repeated it in Spanish for the benefit of anyone who might have missed it in English. From then on, plans moved swiftly.

In brief, General agreed to invest about $85,000 for a 20 per cent interest in a new company to be formed to take the place of El Popo and General's branch operation. In return General was to get its share of the dividends that might result from a successful operation, and also was to be paid a technical service fee. After the first year the new company began to show profits and, in 1934, General's first income from technical service was $22,305.74.

W.O. and President Rodriguez grew to be good personal friends. On several occasions the President was the houseguest of the O'Neils in Akron. W.O. always expressed admiration for the integrity of the Latin American businessman and also for many of the leading politicians who, he thought, were trying their honest best to establish responsible governments despite age-old problems which U.S. politicians do not have to face. Industry in no Latin

American country furnishes a comparable amount of employment—to say nothing of wage rate—so in no other is the tax income from business in any way comparable. Because of the job the best of the Latin American leaders do, despite these two economic deficiencies, they deserve more credit than they usually get.

W.O. maintained that the Latin American standards of honesty and trustworthiness were high. As an example he cited the fact that sometimes after General and El Popo began their operations, General's service fee might have been construed as illegal if the Mexican directors had wanted to seize on a technicality and hide behind the color of the law. But they did not. In fact, they changed the original agreement to spell out more clearly that General's remuneration was a fee for technical service, not a royalty.

W.O. admired the Spanish character and temperament. He felt that Americans, because of our predominantly Anglo-Saxon traditions, did not understand the Spanish. His opinion with respect to them was consistent with his feelings about Latin Americans and was confirmed by experiences in Spain after his foreign-operations plan went into effect there in 1951.

How General got started in Spain is an interesting story. Its formula had been in successful operation in Portugal since 1946. During the war, Spain had confiscated the Continental rubber plant under its enemy-alien property laws. Continental was owned by German interests and was one of the largest rubber companies in Europe. In 1951, the government put up the property for bids, announcing that it was not going to sell necessarily to the highest bidder, but to the one which in its opinion would do the best job for Spain.

General was not the highest bidder. In fact, it was not

a bidder of record. Consistent with its operating plan for these foreign companies, its interest was a minority stock-holding role, so that the majority interest could be held by nationals. The actual bidder was a wealthy and prominent Madrid businessman, Alfredo Aznar, with whom W.O. had only a verbal agreement. There was nothing in writing to specify the amount of stock General would acquire, or at what price, and nothing about the technical service agreement.

Aznar's bid was successful. Two days later he dropped dead. W.O. was notified immediately and flew to Madrid. Aznar's lawyers were courteous, but explained that the matter would have to be decided by Señor Aznar's widow. So W.O. paid a call on Señora Aznar. After extending his sympathy and when the amenities ended, at least to his impatient satisfaction, W.O. turned the conversation to the reason for his call. "Mrs. Aznar," he said, "your husband and I had a verbal agreement to bid on the Continental rubber plant. I have no written proof. The bid merely said the principals and 'others.' I want to tell you that you could sell your husband's successful bid for a profit of at least a million dollars. I have no legal basis for my claim. It was entirely verbal, between your husband and me, and you have no legal obligation to honor it."

"Señor O'Neil," she replied, "my husband's word was as good as any written document. Please do his memory the honor of carrying out the plan exactly as he discussed it with you."

This was another example, W.O. appreciated, of the high standards of integrity inherent in the Spanish character. The operation in Spain has been highly successful from the start. The plant is located at Torrelavega and is known as General Fábrica Española del Caucho, S.A. Eduardo de Aznar y Coste is president and Dr. Jan Piotrowski managing director. In addition to tires and tubes the company produces camelback—the strips of tread rubber used in recapping tires—molded and mechanical rubber goods. It also does a brisk business in repair materials not unlike W.O's original company in Kansas City.

Dr. Piotrowski is a veteran General Tire administrator, knowledgeable and personable. He was also the managing director of General's only unfortunate venture in the foreign field. In 1937, the formula was put into effect in Poland and two plants were in operation when, just two years later, the little country was invaded almost simultaneously by Nazi Germany and Russia. General's plants were in the sector first overrun by the Communists with heavy loss of lives and property. Dr. Piotrowski lived through the inferno and escaped from Poland only after a series of harrowing experiences. He admires the orderly discipline of Spanish life under Franco, whose laws he recognizes as being based on what the Western mind accepts as traditional morality and justice.

W.O. always felt that Franco was the most maligned head of a modern government. He felt that he was the world-wide target of Communist propaganda because he had crushed the attempted Communist takeover of Spain in the three-year Spanish Civil War, from 1936 to 1939. His defeat of the so-called Loyalists was the first major military defeat of a Communist government. "Don't fall for that phony 'Loyalist' tag," W.O. used to say. "They are loyal to nothing that is Spanish, but to whoever is issuing the orders in Moscow."

W.O. was also fond of quoting the high British diplomat who in 1938, the year of the Munich Pact, asked him: "Why are you Americans so critical of Franco? Winston Churchill isn't." To bring this into historical perspective it is necessary to recall that the Spanish Civil War was still in bitter progress; Prime Minister Neville Chamberlain and his umbrella were the symbols of Axis "appeasement," and the loudest anti-Axis voice in Britain was Winston Churchill's.

Churchill was out of office at the time, but his anti-Axis eloquence had begun to shatter Chamberlain's policy. Within a year Chamberlain was forced to appoint him First Lord of the Admiralty, and the following May Churchill became Prime Minister.

Churchill was not critical of Franco because he was enough of a political realist to know that Franco owed a decent amount of gratitude to Mussolini for sending him aid during his death-struggle fight against the Communists in the Civil War still raging in 1938. And Churchill either felt he was a good enough judge of character, or had enough good information, to know that Franco could be depended upon not to cooperate with Hitler. In view of Britain's opinion of the military importance of Gibraltar and the relative ease with which it could be taken from "behind," it is most significant that Churchill never expressed a doubt that Franco would prevent Hitler's armies from crossing the Spanish border and coming upon Gibraltar from the rear.

If Franco had permitted this, Allied control of the Mediterranean would have been lost. Instead, Gilbraltar was still in British hands and fully functional to protect the movement of Allied troops in our African and Italian campaigns.

To those who argued that the Spanish forces were not formidable enough to prevent Hitler's forces from crossing the border, W.O. pointed out that the Pyrenees were a solid deterrent to a panzer advance, and that a relatively small Spanish army dispersed in mountain caves with light artillery could have wrought havoc on armored units lumbering up steep mountain grades, necessarily in single file.

At any rate, the history books are clear on this point: Franco, in the best tradition of the sheriff in the Westerns W.O. loved to read, threatened to shoot it out with any "bad guys" he found trying to come through the pass. And Hitler, who had overrun France, is the only "bad guy" he could have meant.

In most countries, the formula W.O. worked out for the first foreign operation in Mexico has prevailed all through the years to everyone's satisfaction—except the Communists who took over the Polish plants. The standard contract calls for a minority interest for General plus a technical service fee.

In three countries—Germany, Italy, and Japan—only technical service is supplied. Remuneration for this, as in all cases, is based on a percentage of the total business. The rapid and extensive spread of the plan is another example of General's remarkable penchant for profitable proliferation. In this instance, the diversification is country by country.

The plan's phenomenal growth began in the first postwar year, 1946, when W.O.'s youngest brother, the late Cyril F. O'Neil, was elected to head the company's foreign operations. His implementation of W.O.'s ideas, with the world-ranging assistance of Joe Andreoli as vice-president of the export company until his retirement in 1963, created the era—and the new corporate division—of General Tire International.

This is how consistently the plan has grown, especially since 1946:

> 1933 Mexico
> 1937 Poland (two plants shut down by
>   Russian invasion)

1940	Venezuela
1941	Chile
1946	Portugal
1946	Union of South Africa
1949	West Germany
1950	Brazil
1950	Italy
1951	Spain
1952	The Netherlands
1956	Argentina
1956	Guatemala
1957	Japan
1958	Morocco
1963	Ecuador
1963	Pakistan
1964	Iran

General's operations in Canada are carried on through a separate subsidiary company which is not a part of the International complex.

The growth pattern is a tribute to the great teamwork of C. F. O'Neil and Joe Andreoli. At the time of his retirement in 1964, C. F. was president of General Tire International. He had been a longtime director of the company and had joined General Tire in 1919, after World War I, in which he was one of the first fliers in the old Navy Air Corps. He died at his home in Cleveland, Ohio, July 13, 1965.

General's first income from technical service fees was, as we have seen, the $22,305.74 received from the Mexican operation in 1934. Its investment, it will be recalled, for a 20 per cent interest was about $85,000.

In 1964, just eighteen years after the big thrust began, General's foreign investments totaled $18,879,932. Income that year from technical service fees alone was more than two million dollars. This amounted to 12 per cent on the investment, although auditors point out that it cannot really be figured this way because there is no direct connection between the amount of the fees and General's capital investments in the various countries. General's shareholding interest is as low as 15 per cent in some countries, and in others nearly 50 per cent. And the fee is paid not for its investment but for its technical service.

If the production of all the foreign companies is included, General is easily the third largest tire company in the world in units produced. This is not generally realized. Nor is the fact that in some of these countries the production of plastics has begun. Based on General's domestic experience in Chemical/Plastics in recent years, this could have dramatic effects on the growth and profits of General Tire International.

W.O. was always proud of the export technical service agreements. In later years, he referred to them often in talks at the Annual Conferences of domestic dealers. He felt these agreements represented universal recognition of General's know-how—and acknowledgment by rubber authorities all over the world of General's leadership in rubber research.

There is no question that one reason W.O. started to pour more and more of the company's earned surplus into research before World War II was to enhance the value of General's technical services to foreign companies and to make them increasingly attractive.

13

The war years

IN DOLLARS and cents, the war years at General
Tire were not big. This is the way net profits ran after
taxes:

1941	$1,218,570
1942	882,963
1943	1,740,085
1944	2,198,569
1945	1,582,353

The company was called upon to produce a wide variety of products. Some had been experimental, never
before produced in quantity; General's reputation for ver-
satility was put to the test. A new type of gas mask was
an early item. It required intricate molding, which General mastered after several other companies failed. Huge
collapsible pontoons for temporary bridges were another
major item for Army use in combat areas in both the South
Pacific and Europe.

In these years, too, the company built and operated for
the government a munitions plant in Mississippi, and 500-
pound bombs were made in the new mechanical rubber

goods plant at Wabash, Indiana. The Aerojet Engineering Corporation of California—the acquisition of which is described in the next chapter—was beginning to produce JATO units for all branches of the Armed Services. Hundreds of huge barrage balloons were made in a new plant in Akron. The Army used these as decoys, mooring them at strategic locations in combat areas. W.O. loved the story about one barrage balloon which developed a homing instinct. It was shipped to a military establishment about 600 miles to the southwest for inflation and a test mooring. One noon hundreds of General Tire workers on their lunch period were startled to recognize one of their own barrage balloons flying directly over the factory. After a hasty check the Army was notified, and the Coast Guard alerted in Cleveland. In midafternoon a Coast Guard cutter crew on Lake Erie sighted the runaway, brought it down with a high-powered rifle, and retrieved it from the water.

There were literally hundreds of other highly specialized items, ranging from some of the earliest guided missiles to delousing bags. And, of course, there was tremendous pressure to produce all sorts of tires for planes and military vehicles. Civilian passenger-car tire production almost stopped under strict rationing, but W.O.'s battle to establish the drum method of making truck tires provided for military and essential civilian transportation. Without the drum process the production of truck tires would have been a serious bottleneck to the war effort.

As a matter of record, General received its first so-called war order on September 14, 1939. This was just two weeks after the invasion of Poland by Nazi Germany and the Soviet union to begin what developed into World War II. The company was notified by Washington that it had won a contract totaling $4773 to make items needed in the U.S.

"industrial mobilization" program. Much of the total was for rubber bands, leading W.O. to ask at one point whether "the government was getting ready to fight a war with slingshots."

Difficult-to-mold rubber gas masks were ordered in December 1939 by Finland, which was alarmed by its exposed position.

The following year events made more and more apparent the fact that the United States could not avoid the conflict, so a miscellany of military orders began.

General, of course, was called upon for a wide variety of tires for military vehicles and mobile guns. The company also began the manufacture of earphone sets for airplane radios, mounts for gun carriages, inflatable rubber "landing craft" the purpose of which was to decoy German fliers into waste bombings.

Aerojet had begun to produce the JATO rocket, which oddly turned out to be one of the least-known developments in America's arsenal—odd because both Dr. von Kármán and Dr. Fritz Zwicky of Aerojet were internationally known scientists whose work should have been known. And neither von Kármán nor Andrew G. Haley, then president of Aerojet, had made any secret of the product; in fact, they had tried to interest other companies in it before W.O.'s meetings with Haley in New York.

The West Coast operation turned out thousands of rockets of all types. During the 1945 Battle of the Bulge, each day's production was flown immediately to Halifax, Nova Scotia, transferred by ferry planes to England, and then delivered to the combat area. The transportation schedule was so neatly routined that the Germans were hit with General-made rockets within seventy-two hours after they left the assembly line in California. With today's jet planes this schedule could be greatly improved, but at the time it was considered a remarkable bit of coordination.

General's wartime operations in Huntington, West Virginia, and in Cuyahoga Falls, near Akron, turned out complicated and top-secret launching rigs for V–1-type rocket bombs which Allied forces were ready to use as the war ended.

One feature of these launching rigs was that they traveled over hundred-foot railroad tracks and, in that distance, reached a speed of 120 miles per hour. They were made of magnesium, an exotic metal in those days. Few companies knew how to handle it, and General originated many of the basic techniques.

There were many other items which should be mentioned, if only to honor the achievement of the General Tire people who produced them. The complete list is long. It included the previously mentioned barrage balloons, inflatable life vests, life-saving rafts, military raincoats, bulletproof tubes, ammunition, and much more.

One of W.O.'s creative enthusiasms at an early period during the war was for guayule rubber. The guayule shrub grows in wild profusion in most parts of our more arid southwestern regions, especially so in the Mexican State of Coahuila, which borders Texas. Guayule can be processed to yield rubber but had not been used for that purpose since the ancient Aztecs made footballs of it. Somewhere W.O. heard about it and, because of General's good Mexican relations, was able to put in operation an extraction plant in the State of Coahuila. Each guayule shrub contains a minute amount of latex, so the collection problem was enormous. General scientists and production people, however, had no problem working out the extraction process.

The difficulties in connection with collecting sufficient

quantities of guayule shrubs prevented the program from being a full-scale success. However, the rubber produced was of good quality—much better than the original GR-S synthetic—and in those difficult days, with the natural rubber supply of the Far East cut off by the Japanese, any new supply helped. General's guayule rubber could be molded into intricate shapes which the first GR-S proved too stiff to accommodate, but the supply was limited because of the collection problem and, anyway, synthetic-rubber technology moved along rapidly and the need for guayule as a source ended. But it was an imaginative approach, and it actually worked within the limits of the number of plants that could be gathered for processing.

More in the mainstream of the wartime effort to overcome the natural-rubber shortage was General's contributions to the synthetic rubber program. At the time, as just noted, the quality of synthetic rubber was very poor. W.O. felt that what was needed was a crash program of research, plus an increase in new plant facilities, financed by the government. Industry should continue, however, to operate on a competitive, free-enterprise basis to improve the product and meet the demand.

Since 1932, when most manufacturers were still regarding natural rubber as an irreplaceable commodity and continuing to invest in rubber plantations half the world away, W.O. had led his company into a series of important cooperative studies in an attempt to improve the quality of synthetic rubber. General entered into a contract with the Joint American Study Company, Standard Oil of New Jersey, and I. G. Farben of Germany, pioneers of Buna-S, the first synthetic rubber and the one Germany used throughout the war. The Standard Oil Company of New Jersey was the American agent for the I. G. Farben formula, an arrangement later canceled by the war. Under

General's arrangement with Standard Oil and I. G. Farben, a great deal of testing of synthetic rubber on a factory scale was carried on between 1933 and 1939. And a great deal was learned about it.

General carried on much factory-scale testing of synthetic rubber during these years simply because W.O. was intensely interested in developing a satisfactory synthetic to take the place of natural rubber and avoid the wide price fluctuations of that commodity. Incidentally, W.O. tried to avoid the use of the word *synthetic*. All during the war he tried to popularize the term *American rubber,* but he was never successful.

General's first formal research department got under way in 1942. Its purpose was to conduct research in the fields of synthetic-rubber manufacture. Most of the work was done at Akron, but cooperative efforts were entered into with the Sun Oil Company, Carnegie Institute of Technology, Purdue University, and the University of Notre Dame, where Father Julius Nieuwland many years before had made the first synthetic rubber in America on a laboratory scale. This early process of Father Nieuwland used acetylene as a base, and had been sold to E. I. du Pont de Nemours & Co. The product was known first as Duprene, and later as Neoprene.

The acetylene base of the 1930s was outmoded by the later Styrene-Butadiene combination, but from these university and other research programs General learned a great deal—early—about synthetics. It discovered some very effective catalysts, including one making practicable the polymerization of "cold rubber"—recognized at the time as a tremendous step toward the better synthetic rubber that was so badly needed.

In July 1943 General, although not a member of the "rubber pool," at the government's request took over the management of a government-built GR-S plant at Baytown, Texas. This was a management contract only and in no way affected General's position with respect to the pool.

W.O. never did allow General to join the wartime "rubber pool." This had been formed, under government aegis, after a series of hastily called emergency meetings of industry leaders. W.O.'s refusal to be a party to it came after first one and then another major rubber company insisted on holding out certain processes covered by patents. W.O. felt that if the pool idea was necessary as a wartime measure, so was the inclusion of *all* processes for the duration. Unable to win agreement on this point, he emphatically refused to be a party to the pool and never did join it.

Actually, he regarded the pool as the wrong approach anyway. He thought it was a kind of "corporate collectivism" and an invitation to everyone in the industry to sit back and wait for others to make creative improvements and for bureaucratic red tape to get unwound.

General's first great research success after taking over at Baytown came quickly. In 1944 it succeeded, where all others had failed, in developing a process for mixing carbon black with liquid latex and achieving perfect dispersal. Carbon black is the ingredient which gives wearing qualities to tire-tread rubber. Naturally, the more perfectly it is dispersed the better. Prior to 1944, carbon black had to be mixed into the solid rubber, either in the banbury or on the mill, and complete uniformity of dispersion was impossible. General's process, known as latex masterbatching, resulted in an increase of 35 per cent in milling capacity, lowered costs, and a greatly improved rubber compound.

Later, the latex masterbatching process was improved by using HAF (High Abrasion Furnace) carbon black, a process which also went into production at Baytown. The industry as a whole credits General with thus producing another very significant step forward in the development of better GR-S tires, because tread-cracking—a chronic trouble—was greatly reduced. HAF carbon blacks had not had good acceptance in the industry before that because of several technical shortcomings. A less flexible company would not have bothered to experiment with them. But they worked, and well. It was General's latex masterbatching process that for a considerable time made the introduction of HAF blacks possible and gave to other companies the incentive to work out their own methods.

Later, latex masterbatches of pigments, particularly insoluble sulfur and accelerators, to increase the ease and efficiency of their integration with synthetic rubber, were originated. These masterbatches are still being manufactured and sold to other rubber companies by General Tire's Chemical Division.

One of the great frustrations of W.O.'s career was that the government "stayed in the rubber business" many years after the war. The decision whether or not to sell the government-owned plants to private companies became a political football. Due to rapid changes during the war, many of the plants were in various stages of obsolescence by the time the government got around to disposing of them in the mid-1950s. General operated the Baytown plant until July 1955. The batch method of production, which the equipment there provided for, had become obsolete and General decided upon a larger, more efficient continuous-flow facility to be built near Odessa, Texas. A long-term agreement was signed with the El Paso Natural Gas Company to pipe in Styrene and Butadiene, the basic raw materials required, from its nearby refineries. The complex is one of the industry's most efficient producers.

It has developed mostly under the administration of Jerry O'Neil, who became President in 1960, just three years after Odessa had gone onstream and who, as his father's executive assistant, had had a lot to do with its planning.

14

Personal tragedy and Aerojet

THE GREATEST TRAGEDY in Will O'Neil's life occurred on Friday, May 12, 1944. His twenty-five-year-old son Hugh, a Navy pilot and veteran of eight combat missions in the South Pacific, had been rotated back to the Navy base at San Diego, California, to instruct other flyers in aircraft-carrier takeoffs and landings. On this particular afternoon, Lieutenant O'Neil took off from a carrier with two other pilots, each in a separate plane. They were flying a routine pattern about a hundred miles off the coast when suddenly Hugh's plane was forced into the ocean by a mechanical failure. The sea was very rough and the wind high. The pilots of the planes accompanying Hugh saw what had happened. They circled and dropped emergency rubber life rafts. Unfortunately, these landed downwind. In the rough seas, Lieutenant Hugh began to take in a lot of water and, despite his life preserver, drowned while swimming toward the closer raft. Almost simultaneously, from a blimp overhead a young radio man, John Sosnowski, volunteered to go down a rope, carrying a rubber boat and dropping the last fifteen feet. Sosnowski lost his boat in the high waves but succeeded in swimming to Lieutenant Hugh and held his body afloat until a cruiser appeared alongside and took the two aboard. A Navy PBY flying boat also reached the scene within minutes of Hugh's crash, but a high wave damaged its wing upon landing and the PBY was unable to maneuver. The tragedy was particularly heartbreaking because if any of the several life-saving efforts had succeeded, Lieutenant Hugh would have reached the rubber raft safely or would have been rescued.

Hugh's body was returned to Akron. A funeral was held in St. Vincent Church, redolent with so many O'Neil family memories—it had been the parish of Hugh's great-uncle, Father Thomas J. Mahar, the pastor who had introduced Michael O'Neil to his bride-to-be, Patience Mahar, and who had been pastor during most of the years that their children, including W.O., had attended its parochial school.

A few months later, on January 3, 1945, a son, Hugh, Jr., was born to Hugh's widow, Jean Palmer O'Neil, at St. Thomas Hospital, which it will be remembered was first endowed by Michael O'Neil and named in memory of Father Thomas Mahar. The boy inherited his father's sense of duty and tradition of heroism. At nineteen, on July 21, 1964, Hugh, Jr., died in the rescue of two persons caught in the collapse of an Akron street during a cloudburst. Posthumously he was awarded the Carnegie Medal for heroism at the annual dinner meeting of the Akron Chamber of Commerce on February 1, 1965. The Chamber also presented an award of its own. Hughie had completed his freshman year at Georgetown University before his death. He was a graduate of Akron's Hoban High, and his Class of '63 erected and dedicated a flagpole to his memory. On its granite base appears this inscription:

In Memory of Hugh O'Neil, Jr., 1945–64. Hugh in order to save the lives of others gave up his life. His act of Christian courage expresses the highest ideals of the Hoban man. His classmates and friends erect this memorial in his honor. Greater love than this no man has that one lay down his life for his friends.

Lieutenant Hugh's death off the coast of San Diego affected W.O. deeply. He had four other sons, three of them lieutenants in various branches of the service. The oldest, Bill, was president of radio station WJW in Cleveland. Tom was the skipper of an LST in the South Pacific and a beachmaster for part of this time. John was with the Coast Guard in Air-Sea Rescue and Anti-Submarine Warfare Service. Michael G. (Jerry) was an Army flight instructor. Their only sister, Grace, was graduated from Mahattanville College, Purchase, New York, during the month of Hugh's funeral.

W.O. realized that he was not alone in his grief as the father of a pilot who had lost his life in the war. A short time before, Sam Poor, Jr., had been killed in a plane crash in the South Pacific. Sam's father was the General Tire vice-president, formerly Grace O'Neil's bridge partner when W.O. teamed up with Bill Coughlin or some other visiting dealer in the early days. And there were many, many others.

Within a few months of Hugh's death, a remarkable series of coincidences led O'Neil to an interest in the work of a small group of scientists in California who had formed a company to produce the only device in the world that could have taken Hugh's rescue plane off the water, had its wing tip not been damaged.

[156]

According to those close to W.O. at the time, the tragedy had no connection with W.O.'s sudden decision to purchase a 50 per cent interest in the Aerojet Engineering Corporation of Pasadena instead of a radio station he had intended to buy. Because of the timing, however, there are those who wonder whether there was a connection. After all, W.O.'s thought processes were intricate. He also had a secret, introspective side and could keep his own counsel.

Regardless of motive, the facts surrounding the formation of Aerojet in 1942 and its eventual affiliation with General Tire in 1944 are fascinating and complex. The cast of characters and the circumstances had a bizarre, Alice-in-Wonderland quality in keeping with the unreal world of rocketry in the early 1940s.

The Aerojet Engineering Corporation was the commercial outgrowth of a university research program begun in 1937 in the Guggenheim Aeronautical Laboratory of the California Institute of Technology (GALCIT) under the distinguished Dr. Theodore von Kármán, to whom President John F. Kennedy presented the first National Medal of Science on February 18, 1963.

Born in Budapest, Hungary, in 1881, von Kármán was an authentic child prodigy. By the time he was six, he could multiply five-digit numbers in his head. He learned to speak a half-dozen languages—"all with a Hungarian accent," by his own admission. In 1930, he emigrated to America because he anticipated the Nazi tyranny.

During his long lifetime—he died at the age of eighty-one on May 6, 1963—von Kármán earned twenty-four honorary degrees, ten decorations, thirty-two awards, and belonged to thirty-three scientific societies. He was called "The Einstein of Aviation," "The Father of Supersonic Flight," and "The Patron of the U.S. Air Forces." His military friend was General of the Armies H. H. (Hap) Arnold, wartime Army Air Forces chief. Most scientists credit von Kármán and General Arnold for the research-and-development orientation of the modern U.S. Air Forces.

Perhaps von Kármán's closest friend in Aerojet was T. Edward Beehan, who joined the company in 1942, a few months after it was founded. He became an officer in 1943 and a director in 1945. A tall, urbane, impeccably dressed native of Providence, Rhode Island, and a Phi Beta Kappa graduate of Brown University, Beehan was the visual and temperamental opposite of von Kármán, who was the archetype of the Old-World absent-minded professor, but the relationship between the two was very close. At von Kármán's request, Beehan served as the administrator of his estate and that of his sister Josephine (Pipo), who had died in 1951. Von Kármán, who never married, lived with Pipo; she supervised most of his personal life. Because of their close association, Beehan told many stories about this colorful genius as well known for wit and eccentricity as for his brilliant discoveries in aerodynamics. Once when talking to a pretty girl pilot, von Kármán explained that a tailspin is "something like a love affair; you don't notice how you get into it, and it is very hard to get out of." He defined a Hungarian as "a man who goes in a revolving door behind you and comes out ahead." His absent-mindedness was severe. He left a trail of forgotten hats, coats, and brief cases. During the war, military authorities assigned an officer to gather up the classified documents von Kármán left behind.

In von Kármán's home one evening, Beehan made a tape recording which has considerable historic interest. It is an accurate, first-person account of von Kármán's earliest work in this country and of Aerojet's formative years. These are edited excerpts from that tape:

"When I came to this country in 1930, I was invited by the Guggenheim Foundation and the late Dr. Robert Millikan, the Nobel prize-winning physicist at Caltech, to accept the directorship of GALCIT, the forerunner of today's Jet Propulsion Laboratory, at Pasadena, California. Soon thereafter I had the very good fortune to meet General Hap Arnold. At the time he was a lieutenant colonel at March Field. He came to Caltech frequently to see what we were doing. He seemed to enjoy it and we got well acquainted. In about '36 or '37, Arnold encouraged me to have my so-called GALCIT group go to work on rocket research. It was a surprising suggestion because, at that time, very few people took rockets seriously. In fact, it seems to me now that General Arnold was about the only military man who foresaw any future for them.

"If you will look at the history of rockets, a negative view concerning them was somewhat justified. A rocket, as you know, is a very old invention. They say the Chinese used the first ones as weapons. They were really arrows driven by a primitive rocket device in the shaft. During medieval times and until about the beginning of the eighteenth century, a rocket was used as a weapon, but then the rifled gun barrel was invented, greatly increasing the accuracy of firearms, and military men abandoned the rocket altogether. It is a fact that the British General Staff made a decision that the rocket was so inexact that there was no military value in it. That, of course, more or less killed the development of the rocket over two hundred years ago. Isn't it ironic that a device that was thought outmoded in the eighteenth century should in the twentieth century usher in the age of supersonic flight and space exploration?

[159]

"From the beginning of our rocket research at GALCIT, we were not interested in rocket weaponry, but in an application of rocket power which would assist planes to take off from restricted runways and enable rescue planes to take off from the sea.

"Besides myself, our GALCIT group included Frank Malina, a graduate student; Martin Summerfield, also a student of mine; and two young noncollegians, John W. Parsons and Edward S. Forman. These two were town boys who had made a hobby of experimenting with rockets since their teens. At one point in their early career they had obtained permission to use a small laboratory on the Caltech campus, but incurred Dr. Millikan's displeasure by promptly blowing it up. Shortly after that, I took them into our group, which I was just starting because General Arnold told me that I should show the military that college professors are good for something.

"From the start, we were known on the campus as the Suicide Club. We carried on our laboratory work at Caltech and every so often would make a trip out into the country with a few primitive rockets and fire them. Our favorite proving ground was a canyon about the size of a large gravel pit. We were generally regarded as eccentrics, or as children pursuing a dangerous, foolish hobby.

"Our first practical success came in August 1941, when a light plane equipped with six of our JATO rockets was lifted from a runway at March Air Force Base. Each contained two pounds of black powder and cornstarch to make the mixture a propellant and not an explosive.

"I don't remember who coined the name JATO—from the initial letters of Jet-Assisted Take Off—but it went into the history of technology and became familiar to everyone during World War II like the word *Jeep*.

"With the success of our first practical test behind us,

Malina, Summerfield, Parson, Forman, and I began talking among ourselves about what our next step should be. We were not businessmen, and we thought the production should be turned over to an industrial company. One of the big airplane manufacturers seemed most logical and I had contacts with them since I was director of the Guggenheim Laboratory and chief of the wind tunnel. We were unsuccessful, however, in finding any company who could be interested. So we decided to found our own company, but we still hoped to find some manufacturer who would take over the production on a licensing basis. The Aerojet Engineering Corporation was incorporated on March 20, 1942. The five of us in the GALCIT group each put in $250, so we began with the tremendous capital of $1250. The incorporation papers were drawn up by Andrew G. Haley, a Washington, D.C., attorney, whom I had met the year before under trying personal circumstances. My sister, Pipo, had been in America as long as I had been, but unlike me had neglected to take out citizenship papers. For many years she had taught Romance languages at the University of Southern California and now, with war clouds gathering, we both became alarmed about her Hungarian citizenship. A friend of mine in the Bureau of Aeronautics at Washington suggested that I bring Pipo's problem to Mr. Haley. He handled this matter efficiently, so it was natural that I should ask him to draw up the papers for our new company and to act as our attorney.

"The incorporation papers drawn up by Haley named me as president of the company, but by fall of that year, 1942, it was obvious that the practical problems of running the business were incompatible with my scientific work. I called a meeting of the other stockholders and proposed that I become technical advisor and that Haley be elected president.

"This was done on September 23, 1942, but by this time Haley, who had been a major in the reserves, had been called into active duty and was attached to the Judge Advocate General's office. I called General Arnold at five o'clock in the morning, California time, when it was eight in Washington, and told him he had a man I needed. He replied, 'O.K. What division is he in?' I shall never forget his reaction when I answered, 'He works for the Judge Advocate General.' 'The Judge Advocate General!' he shouted. 'Why the hell do you need a lawyer? Some engineers I can understand, but why a lawyer?' I explained the situation we were in, and that we needed legal, financial, and practical business guidance badly; that Haley had worked with us in organizing the company, knew a good deal about what we were doing and was the logical one to help us. General Arnold worked swiftly. At 11 A.M., Washington time, Haley was called into the office of the Secretary of War and given a letter releasing him from duty 'in the interest of the Armed Services' so he could come to Aerojet."

Aerojet's first location was in a former fruit-juice plant on Colorado Street in Pasadena. The second was not much better. It was a building that had been a car dealer's showroom and service quarters. The offices were in the salesrooms and experimental production began in what had been the service area. The building was in an urban neighborhood, a location wholly unsuited to the exotic business of mixing rocket propellants and packing them into metal containers that were the first production JATO units. There was no place to test the units, and reasonable quality-control standards required frequent test by actual firings. So, late in 1942, one acre of ground in a sparsely settled section of Azusa, California, was leased as a testing ground. Almost immediately, with Air Force endorsement, negotiations were begun with the Defense Plant Corporation for the construction of a rocket pilot plant on forty-eight acres adjacent to the new Azusa testing ground. The Air Force regarded the new facility as extremely important to the war effort because JATO units were proving successful in carrier takeoffs and in rescue operations by amphibious planes. An initial appropriation of $149,000 was received from the Defense Plant Corporation. Negotiations for building the pilot plant were prolonged because the DPC believed that $200 an acre was a fair price for the property, and the $210 asked by the owner, the Azusa Land & Water Co., was too high. For a total possible saving of $480 on the land, initial production at Azusa was delayed about sixty days, while the war went on.

Soon the demand for the JATO units and for liquid-rocket motors which the Navy and Air Force were extremely interested in developing made immediate plant expansions necessary and required seven additional appropriations totaling over $2 million.

By the summer of 1943, Aerojet's number of employees had increased from the original half-dozen to 250, and by the spring of 1944 had passed 600. But as its research projects became more diversified and sophisticated, its personnel and production problems increased. Aerojet was not a factory, it was an intellectual Tower of Babel. A high percentage of its personnel were university-oriented scientists with no previous experience in industry. Most of them were individualistic, some quite eccentric. One especially brilliant scientist captured a snake which he found slithering across the testing ground one day and then wore it around the office. His live necktie caused a devastating turnover in secretarial help. A more serious deterrent to steady production was the fact that rocketry was so new that the creative minds of the scientists were forever finding new technical ways of achieving the same practical results. The solid-propellant JATO finally became fairly stabilized in basic design, and sufficient production was achieved in 1943 to catapult the company into international prominence.

The scientific quest for constant improvement went on, however, both on the JATO unit and particularly in the development of liquid-propellant rocket motors, a highly sophisticated field in which Aerojet led from the beginning, and in the field of broad basic research in underwater devices and propellants under the direction of Dr. Fritz Zwicky, internationally renowned astrophysicist of the California Institute of Technology.

Most of this research proved of great scientific value and was encouraged by the Navy and Air Force, but it had a highly unfavorable effect on JATO production. The first great test came in 1943, with the receipt of an Air Force order for $2.7 million worth of JATO units, all to be delivered by December 31. The contract date was met, but just barely. The order was completed on the last day of the year. Haley, Beehan, Bill Zisch (then assistant treasurer and later president) and others in the office worked a full night shift in the production department all during December, after their regular daytime duties. They spent Christmas Day in the shipping department.

Meeting that first production contract by a whisker gave the Aerojet management cause for concern. There was temporary exhilaration over meeting the contract date for the first big order, but Haley, in particular, realized that a great deal more financing and industrial management ability was necessary before further large-scale contracts could be undertaken. In fact, the military insisted on these as a condition of future contracts. The Navy and Air Force talked informally but insistently in terms of contracts totaling $30 million to $50 million. Haley's outsize laboratory, where production was looked upon as something of a nuisance, could not finance production on that scale. Von Kármán had failed to interest any of his aviation-company contacts, so Haley went East to seek help. He needed financing, but he also needed the management skills of a company acceptable to the Navy and Air Force. In his pocket was a list of ten companies the military would accept.

When he reached New York there occurred the remarkable coincidence which was responsible for General Tire's first association with Aerojet.

W.O. was in New York with his radio attorney from Washington, W. Theodore Pierson. W.O. and Grace stopped at the Plaza, Ted Pierson at the St. Regis. The first afternoon they were in town was cold and blustery, early in 1944. W.O. took Grace on a shopping expedition to a Fifth Avenue store near the hotel. His usual zest for such a trip was dulled by tire rationing, which prevented his selling the president of the store a set of General tires, as was his custom. He settled for haggling a discount on Grace's purchases.

While W.O. was thus occupied, Ted Pierson had nothing to do until his dinner appointment that evening with W.O. at the Lotus Club. He took a walk. Rounding the St. Regis corner, at Fifty-fifth Street, Pierson met Haley coming up Fifth Avenue.

"My first quick impression was that Andy looked preoccupied and depressed," Pierson recalled later. "We were old friends. Andy had been my boss at the FCC some years before. Then we went into private practice together, specializing in radio law in Washington, and dissolved our partnership about the time that Andy took care of Dr. von Kármán's sister's immigration problem. We continued to be good friends, practicing separately, with Andy spending more and more of his time on the Coast with Aerojet. We hadn't seen each other in a long time; had a great deal to reminisce about, and the blustery corner was not conducive to a good conversation, so I invited him into the King Cole Room of the St. Regis for a cocktail.

"Once inside and seated, Andy began to tell me about his experiences with Aerojet, his present crisis, and his fears for the future of the company. He pulled out of his pocket the sheet of paper on which was typed the ten major companies, any one of which he hoped might help him. General Tire was on the list. He asked me if I was still doing legal work for Bill O'Neil and I replied that I was; that we were, in fact, in town together, and having dinner that evening at the Lotus Club. I invited him to join us and he accepted. That was the gist of our conversation about Aerojet, and we separated to meet later at the Club."

Years later, Pierson recalled that he regarded Haley's rocket company a "Buck Rogers project" and was not interested in it, nor did he believe that W.O. would be. When he phoned W.O. in his room at the Plaza to tell him that he had invited Haley to dinner with them, he explained that he did so partly because Haley was the attorney for the radio station in Boston which W.O. was interested in acquiring.

"I also told W.O. that Haley wanted to talk about his buzz-bomb enterprise in California and asked him to be nice to Haley because of the Boston situation. As far as the latter suggestion was concerned, I could have saved my breath. Before the first martini arrived, Haley was off and running on the subject of Aerojet. He never stopped talking about it, except to answer W.O.'s questions—and they were interested questions. It suddenly came to me, as something of a shock, that W.O. was genuinely interested. The martinis, dinner, and conversation went on for, I suppose, at least three hours, and in all that time there wasn't a word mentioned about the Boston radio station, in which I knew W.O. had a great interest.

"We finally broke up and W.O. asked me to come up to the Plaza for breakfast in the morning. He specified an early hour and I recall that we were the first ones in the Oak Room. We were no sooner seated than W.O. started questioning me about Haley. I remember one question he asked was whether he was a 'crazy Irishman.' I thought this an odd characterization, coming from W.O. The point is that W.O. was obviously fascinated by Haley and his story of the rocket project. I told him that Haley was an excellent lawyer, whom I knew best as a radio specialist, and could vouch for him as a gentleman, but that I knew nothing at all about the merits of Aerojet. That I had wanted him to meet Haley principally to establish a rapport with him because he was the lawyer for the Boston radio station. But there was no switching W.O. to radio. 'He might have something,' W.O. said, and added, 'I'm going to call Dan Kimball to find out.'"

With that, according to Ted Pierson, W.O. left the table and went to the lobby to place a call for Kimball, who was then in charge of General Tire's office in Washington. Kimball, who made a lifetime habit of being at work at dawn, answered the call himself because his staff had not yet arrived. W.O. asked him for information about Aerojet from Navy and Air Force contacts as quickly as possible.

Pierson believes it was before lunch when Kimball called back, reaching W.O. in his hotel room. The gist of Kim-

[167]

ball's report was "Aerojet looks great, W.O. Buy it if you can. Both the Navy and Air Force want a mass production of JATO units, but they know that Aerojet hasn't adequate financing and needs big-league management. Until they are assured on these two points contracts for from thirty to fifty million will be withheld."

Based on this information from Dan Kimball, W.O. decided to go ahead. There is some evidence that W.O. originally thought that General's role could be similar to its unique method of operating in the international field—furnishing a limited investment, extension of credit and management services in return for a fee based on profits. In fact, that is how General did enter Aerojet—technically as a subcontractor to manufacture and to finance the metal parts on a Navy contract for $4 million worth of JATO units. The fee, including reimbursement for financing and management, was to be 50 per cent of the profits. W.O. assigned a great two-man team to head Aerojet—Dan Kimball and Art Rude, General's dealer in Los Angeles and an outstanding businessman.

The metal parts of the JATO had caused most of the trouble in filling the Air Force contract the year before. The cylinders had to withstand terrific internal pressures and required constant quality controls. General solved this metal-parts problem quickly, but the Aerojet operation soon became much more complex. The financial resources required made General's role as a subcontractor inadequate.

W.O.'s interest in Aerojet was intensified as a result of a visit he made to the Azusa plant not long after his talk with Haley in New York. When he returned to Akron, his conversation indicated that he was interested in everything he had seen and heard, from how the town got its name—"It means from A to Z, U.S.A."—to the approximate time required theoretically to rocket the average passenger car from Akron to Cleveland, Ohio. For a while, this illustration became one of W.O.'s conversational devices to make rocket power comprehensible to his tire associates. From his talks with Dr. von Kármán, Dr. Zwicky, and other scientists he had caught the dream of the scientific possibility of rocketing an object out of the earth's gravitational pull and sending it into orbit. He believed that this would be done some day and that Aerojet would build the rocket. In 1944 not very many persons even knew this theory, much less believed in its practicability.

The most important result of W.O.'s first visit to Aerojet, however, was an idea—an informed hunch. In his own mind, after talking with the scientists and inspecting the physical layout, he found a similarity between JATO-propellant chemistry and synthetic-rubber chemistry. He concluded that much rubber-production equipment could be adapted to increase the efficiency of propellants production. W.O. did not say much about this, but he sent for General's research director from Akron, Gilbert Swart, who confirmed W.O.'s theory and also said that a rubber compound would be superior in some formulas to the asphalt being used as a binder.

In December 1944, after W.O.'s visit, General acquired a 50 per cent stock interest in Aerojet for $75,000. This proved one of the most spectacularly successful business purchases of modern times. Only W.O. had the imagination to become intrigued by the idea of it and had the courage to become financially involved. Participation had been offered without success by Dr. von Kármán to other companies more likely to be interested than a tire company might logically be expected to be. Too, General supplied $9 million in financing during the first year.

After the war in Europe, Haley resigned as president of

Aerojet. Those who had called the enterprise "the buzz-bomb factory" were convinced that Aerojet was through. Actually, the company made no money during the war, although by the end of the conflict it was delivering 10,000 JATO units a month to the Armed Services. These had made possible a number of spectacular rescue missions at sea and in the Arctic and on South Pacific islands with airstrips too short for planes not equipped with JATO units to take off after landing.

Also before the war ended, W.O., in a talk much shorter than the Gettysburg Address but memorable to those who heard it, told a formal board of high military officers what he thought of their insistence on developing a "smokeless" JATO unit before continuing JATO production. In colorful language and in his most forceful manner, he said: "Listen. Let me tell you admirals something. The Chinese invented gunpowder centuries ago, but smokeless powder wasn't invented until the Americans did it fifty years ago. The so-and-sos who stuck with bows and arrows waiting for smokeless powder to get invented got the daylights kicked out of them. Do you want to be a bow-and-arrow Navy?"

The Navy decided not to wait. Aerojet was instructed to produce 10,000 JATO units a month. In 1949 a smokeless formula was discovered. This development was too late for the war, but W.O. was satisfied that General Tire know-how had bettered the 600-year quest for smokeless gunpowder. The Navy acknowledged the contributions of the smoky workhorse JATO. The Certificate of Achievement for contributions to naval aviation contained this citation: "The primary contribution was the development, construction, and production of JATO units which were successfully used in the rescue of thousands of wounded disabled personnel in combat areas." Thousands of JATO units were used routinely in carrier takeoffs in the South Pacific.

Except for their obvious adaptability for rescue operations at sea and for takeoffs from carriers and "jungle airstrips," JATO units were not regarded by W.O. as military hardware. He envisioned many peacetime uses. In Mexico City and other high-altitude airports in South America he had seen heavy planes take off with difficulty in thin atmosphere. He visualized a market for JATO units in this service, especially for air-freight planes until passengers could be educated to accept their rather frightening, noisy, smoky swoosh. He also believed that they could be mounted backward and bring a landing plane to a quicker stop—as indeed they could, if planes were completely redesigned for the purpose. He felt that they could be mounted—again backward—on railroad trains, for faster emergency stops than by brakes on wheels.

W.O. expected the thousands of returning pilots to spark a much larger market for private planes than actually developed. He thought each of these single-engine planes should have a JATO unit under the fuselage, capable of instantaneous ignition by pressing a button on the instrument panel, for use in case of engine failure or stalling on takeoff or landing. The effect would be to lift a light plane to an altitude of several thousand feet, from which it could be glided safely back to the runway. W.O. thought JATO units of this type—about the size of a hand-held fire extinguisher—would become standard equipment on light planes, as universal as spare tires on automobiles.

He had many other imaginative uses for JATO units— ideas the practicability of which no one ever successfully refuted. The only ones which materialized were for cargo planes operating out of high-altitude airports and for a limited number of private planes.

[171]

In the postwar years, General increased its 50 per cent interest in Aerojet. The little university experiment of the early 1940s became a subsidiary of General Tire. The name Aerojet Engineering Corporation was changed to Aerojet-General in 1953 because W.O. thought there was no sales appeal in the word *engineering*.

The full story of Aerojet-General's fabulous postwar proliferation into many different fields can merely be outlined within the scope of this story. Hundreds of distinguished scientists contributed to the success of the company—and through it to the security of the nation; to its defense as well as to better peacetime living. Some of these men are recognized as the highest authorities in their sophisticated specialties. Several scientific papers have described their important discoveries and techniques, ranging from new structural materials and their uses to such highly advanced research projects as the unique technological breakthrough which obtains oxygen from rocks on the moon. Balancing this exotic feat are other scientific achievements with widespread commercial application to modern living. Chosen at random from a list that is never complete, these include revolutionary food-processing methods, alternators for the automotive industry, large-scale desalination of sea water at reasonable cost, and industrial chemicals which can be produced less expensively by a nuclear process called fissio-chemistry.

Aerojet's major activities include rocket engines, nuclear auxiliary power systems, power-conversion equipment, astronics, advanced electronics, and guidance systems, marine technology and antisubmarine warfare, chemical, optics, automated warehousing and handling equipment, architect-engineering-construction management, instrumentation and controls fabrication, heavy manufacturing, ordnance and new methods of explosive forming of metals and other materials, surveillance drones, advanced space-mission planning, warning and detection equipment, life sciences, structural materials, and research into the development of other new materials for a myriad of uses in everyday life.

In the rocket field, Aerojet-General still produces JATO units for both military and private aircraft. But it is now primarily known for its larger engines—liquid, solid, and nuclear—for space vehicles such as Titan, Minuteman, Polaris, Apollo, Gemini, M–1, and NERVA. These engines represent an accumulation of scientific and manufacturing know-how that has multiplied geometrically since JATO units began—the "tin lizzies" of the Space Age.

Aerojet-General's tremendous growth and diversification have inspired lyrical descriptions from business writers. *Time* magazine has called the company "The General Motors of Rocketry." The organization has grown from the original GALCIT group of five to a payroll of around 30,000, with more scholastic degrees in science and engineering than any university. For three days after hostilities ceased at the end of World War II, the enterprise was completely out of business, all its contracts having been canceled. It has recovered to make brilliant contributions to practically every space age program, and with its highly diversified activities does an annual business of more than a half-billion dollars, President William E. Zisch points out. His first office job in 1938 was at California Institute of Technology as secretary to Dr. von Kármán and Dr. Clark Millikan, then associate professor of aeronautics. He was twenty years old then. By the time von Kármán had formed Aerojet, Zisch was Caltech's business manager and von Kármán dragooned him into giving a few hours a day to the company. As Aerojet's problems deepened, Zisch became more interested in them, and on

[173]

November 18, 1942, he left Caltech to become Aerojet's full-time manager. He was then twenty-four. He has an amazing ability to live with details and not be overpowered by them. His thinking remains creative. He echoes what Dr. von Kármán once told William O'Neil at one of their first meetings. "General Tire showed a tremendous amount of business courage and vision when it put nine million dollars into expanding Aerojet in that first year, back in 1945, when no other company could be found that had any faith in us at all. We are happy it has worked out so well, and in this Space Age there are still many new worlds to conquer."

15

"That Tom, he makes money"

No GENERAL TIRE field of diversification mystifies the public quite so much as its large-scale operations in radio and television. In its Fiftieth Anniversary year, General had been in radio for twenty-three years, nearly half its corporate life. Nevertheless, the fact that a tire company is the largest independent radio and TV organization in the United States strikes most people as incongruous. Understanding the CBS Network's purchase of the Yankee Baseball Club is elementary by comparison.

For those who like their economics simple, General's expansion into the radio field—which soon added TV—is not an easy exercise in finger-counting arithmetic; it is for those who get a special elation from the success of a soaring idea. The move was one of W.O.'s best.

Perhaps the strangest aspect was the long period of deliberation that preceded W.O.'s action in the matter. We have seen that his first exposure to the medium was in the early 1930s as a sponsor of the Jack Benny show. At that time he made a point of learning a good deal about the business and he liked it. He did nothing, however, which may have been because he was weighing an investment in radio against starting a mechanical rubber goods division. The early and mid-1930s were no time to be impulsive with money.

What influenced W.O. to take the first modest, tentative step into radio was the decision of his oldest son Bill, then twenty-three and only two years out of Holy Cross. All the O'Neils went into business early, and young Bill was no exception. But he wanted to enter radio. Upon hearing that, W.O.'s reaction must have been like that of the Irish father whose daughter mentions at the family dinner table that she'd like to learn to play the harp.

W.O. knew just the station Bill could buy—if he was willing to use the $60,000 in trust funds W.O. and Grace had established for him, as they had for the other five children. Young Bill was willing. The station, WJW, a small one in Akron, was losing money. It had been brought to his attention by his public relations man, Jack Reed.

So young Bill bought the station with his trust fund. The first year he netted a very small profit on the $60,000 investment, but in a year or two he was making a handsome return. Investing more capital into the property, Bill moved the station to Cleveland, where it quickly became a profitable metropolitan major. A Muzak subsidiary was added, supplying piped-in music to offices, factories, restaurants, stores, and other outlets. This service also became profitable, so Bill kept it, but he sold Station WJW in 1950 to the Storer Broadcasting Company when an attractive price was offered. Bill is married and has two sons. He and Mrs. O'Neil live in Miami Beach, Florida, and St. Thomas, Virgin Islands. Bill has radio stations in both places and ranching interests in Montana.

With an assist from the imaginative and gregarious Jack

[176]

Reed, young Bill, in 1942, discovered the Yankee Network deal which introduced and established General Tire in the radio and television business. Yankee was America's fifth largest network, comprised of headquarters outlet WNAC in Boston, stations in Worcester, Providence, and Bridgeport, and twenty-two network affiliates. Station WNAC had recently lost its NBC affiliation and the network was reportedly losing prestige. It was owned by eighty-year old John Shepard, Jr., a New England department-store and real estate magnate whose fortune was estimated at more than $20 million. He had one son, John Shepard III, then in his late fifties, who ran the network; he also had a serious inheritance tax problem.

Young Bill went to Boston and called on the Shepards. He pointed out that if the company bought Yankee it planned to keep the same management team. It had been thought that Bill would assume command, but he had other plans.

In the fall of 1942, Bill O'Neil introduced his father to the elder Shepard. He left the two alone and the deal was concluded. For some years Bill believed his father had paid $1,150,000, but he learned ultimately that the exact figure was $1,175,000. The decision was made by W.O. without the concurrence of his board of directors. It proved a sound purchase. In 1944, Yankee netted $418,000 after taxes, and the entire investment paid out in four years. The stations in Worcester, Providence, and Bridgeport were sold, but the Boston property alone, WNAC and WNAC-TV, is conservatively appraised at $23 million.

Even before 1942, when he disclaimed in his conversation with Shepard any personal interest in an association with the Yankee Network, young Bill O'Neil had decided on a career outside the General Tire complex. Following W.O.'s purchase of Yankee—the legal date was the last day of 1942—Shepard directed the network.

Meanwhile W.O.'s second Kansas City-born son, Thomas F., two years Bill's junior, was serving a long hitch in the South Pacific, most of the time as commander of an LST. Before the war he had been a General territory salesman on the West Coast, under two of the best tutors in the General Tire school of salesmanship—Art Rude, whose Los Angeles dealership was the largest west of Chicago, and Dan Kimball, West Coast manager. Both Rude and Kimball later played major roles in the Aerojet-General saga, and Tom was to be the sparkplug of the big radio-TV diversification. None of the three knew then what diversification lay ahead. Tom was happy selling tires and was a good salesman, especially in selling to the big trucking companies that run up and down the Coast. But he wanted additional experience, and when the managership of the Washington, D.C., office opened, Tom was given the job, leaving it to enter the service. After the war he managed the General Tire store in Boston.

All this time Yankee, while successful, was not subject to any particular General Tire "know-how," as W.O. loved to call whatever it was that caused his organization's efforts to click so well. Tom, however, had been keeping an eye on the radio operation, much as W.O. had done for his father in the case of the Worcester cotton mill. Tom saw TV coming. He wanted to get into radio, which he was sure would expand into TV, the entertainment field, and maybe movies.

In 1947, Tom O'Neil moved from the tire store on Commonwealth Avenue to the posts of vice-president and director of the Yankee Network. The morale of the radio people in those days was mixed. Some of them pulsed with anticipation over the promise of television; to others TV was a threatening specter to be derided and fought. Some were sure it would kill radio, others felt that it would broaden radio's scope of public service and profits. The situation was like the days when sound was added to motion pictures, except that the process was in reverse. Pictures were to be added to sound.

If any man was suited to the dynamics of the new television business, Tom was. Ox, they had called him at Holy Cross, because of his six foot four and 220 pounds. In temperament and energy he more nearly resembled one of his 50,000-watt transmitters. An idea man like his father, he was impatient with the delays that accompanied the first steps in the development of TV transmission.

He remembers that most of the experimental work was done in 1948, and it was a great event in Boston when two small-screen TV sets in the Jordan-Marsh department store picked up the first experimental programs from Station WNAC-TV. For weeks, awed crowds pressed around the receivers.

Tom recalls that year as an artistic success but a financial fiasco. Before the horrendous news could reach W.O., Tom decided to return to Akron and prepare his father for the blow.

As usual, what with visiting dealers, department heads, and assorted old friends of various categories, walking into W.O's office unannounced, to borrow one of his Parliament cigarettes or to get a decision, Tom had difficulty getting his father's undivided attention, let alone the privacy he thought his news deserved. Finally, getting W.O.'s ear, he said: "Dad, I'm afraid we're going to lose about $109,000 this month." "What are you bragging about?" W.O. retorted. "We can lose $750,000 around here in a month."

Normally W.O. would not have taken such a cavalier

attitude toward a loss, but sometime later Tom realized why his father had reacted as he did. First, W.O. had come to have great faith in the future of television. Second, he knew that large sums must be poured into research and development in any new field. He later told a close associate that he thought all the money invested "was a small price to pay for the education we got in TV, as early as we got it, in 1949."

General Teleradio became RKO-Teleradio in 1955 and RKO General in 1959, after a succession of brilliant mergers and acquisitions. Included were the purchase of the Don Lee Network of forty-five stations on the West Coast in 1950, and a 90 per cent interest in Metropolitan New York's bellwether stations—WOR-AM and WOR-TV —from R. H. Macy & Co., in 1952, to be followed by full ownership in 1955.

At one point the Don Lee negotiations were highlighted by a typical W.O. move. The Los Angeles television station, KHJ-TV, was involved. The new owners decided to retain title to the physical assets of the station, but to sign a ten-year lease arrangement with CBS for the station's operation. The deal was complicated and Tom O'Neil was in the office of Dr. Frank Stanton, President of CBS, to conclude the negotiations. As the papers were about to be signed, Stanton handed him the telephone. It was a call from Tom's father. "Tom, do you know the rent CBS is going to pay us is not enough?" W.O. asked. "No," Tom answered. "How much is it?" "I don't know, but it's not enough."

Today, RKO General owns and operates AM radio stations in New York, Boston, Washington, Windsor, Ontario (Detroit market coverage), Los Angeles, San Francisco, and Memphis. It also has a UHF station in Hartford, Connecticut, which is experimenting with a long-term subscription TV test utilizing a "decoder" system developed by Zenith Radio Corporation.

The VHF-TV stations are located in Boston, Los Angeles, New York, Windsor, Ontario (Detroit), and Memphis.

RKO General, therefore, has its statutory maximum of radio stations (seven) and VHF-TV stations (five), so growth, which in any other business would come through adding more and more "stores," is cut off by government edict. The fact that the "Detroit" stations, CKLW and CKLW-TV, are located in Canada raises the interesting question as to whether they count toward the total allowed under one ownership, but no one at RKO General wants to discuss it much.

Tom is more interested in "horizontal" avenues of expansion into all sorts of nonmanufacturing or service businesses. He was among the first to appreciate the true relationship of RKO General to General Tire and Aerojet-General. Tom's view is that General Tire and Aerojet-General, with their many divisions, obviously are large and tremendously diversified manufacturing operations. They maintain costly research-and-development programs, have huge capital plant investments, maintain large inventories, and meet payrolls for more than 50,000 employees. Tom believes RKO General should seek investments for its earnings which avoid the high fixed costs of a manufacturing company and, in the case of a General Tire subsidiary, would likely duplicate existing facilities.

The quest for businesses—"faced to the future," a familiar O'Neil phrase—has already begun, and a number that meet Tom's service concept are successfully under way. Oddly enough, and apparently with no sentiment involved, one phase of the search ended in the heart of his father's old Southwest tire-jobber territory, where W.O. first dreamed the General Tire "proposition."

In April 1961 RKO General bought Video Independent Theaters, Inc., with headquarters in Oklahoma City. The corporation owns or operates 128 theaters in Oklahoma, New Mexico, and Texas. An interesting subsidiary with great growth potential is the Vumore Company, which owns and operates fifteen community antenna installations serving more than 40,000 homes. Another subsidiary is Mesa Microwave, a licensed communications carrier for the relay and transmission of TV signals by microwave. Included in the property is a system of piped-in background music similar to Bill's in Cleveland, and a half-interest in two electronics companies—Electronics International, Inc., and International Crystal Manufacturing Co.

In 1958 Video Independent Theaters, Inc., gained national attention when it conducted "telemovies" tests in Bartlesville, Oklahoma. This first pay-TV test in the United States used a cable system. It failed. Among the reasons were the cost of installations, lack of cooperation from movie theaters which refused to rent first-run movies for the test, and the fact that the service was made available only for a flat monthly fee.

The Bartlesville test first sparked Tom O'Neil's interest in pay-TV. But he determined to approach the problem in a different way when he selected Hartford, Connecticut, for the experiment and was licensed to conduct it beginning June 29, 1962.

RKO General's only UHF station, WHCT, televises four hours of pay-TV every evening, with additional hours on Saturday and Sunday afternoons. The signals are airborne, as in commercial TV, and "unscrambled" on any subscriber's ordinary TV set when a Zenith decoder is activated properly. The program fare is 85 per cent first-run movies, at a cost of one dollar to a dollar and a half for as many viewers as are available to each set at the time of tune-in. No patient in the postoperative ward of a hospital is kept under stricter statistical observation than a Hartford subscription TV patron. Some people might pay the ten-dollar charge of installing the decoder and the seventy-five-cent-a-week rental charge just to have a big company take so much interest in them. Conversely, the 5000 customers have a closer rapport with the station than most people, unfortunately, have with their church. The decoder meters tell the station that viewers sometimes disguise their true tastes. Televising the Bolshoi Ballet, for instance, was heralded as a civic cultural triumph, but only 28 per cent of the audience viewed it. In other words, only 1400 of the 5000 sets were tuned in. The first Clay–Liston heavyweight boxing match, on the other hand, drew an 88 per cent rating—only 600 sets were not tuned in. One man called the station to report proudly that 76 guests in his living room watched the fight. He wondered if anyone had beaten his record. The station was unable to find anyone who had.

Tom O'Neil sees no conflict between pay-TV and commercial TV. "We have had the experiment going long enough in Hartford to know that pay-TV will supplement, not supplant, commercial TV," he says. "The average family viewing in this country is now about forty hours a week. In Hartford, our five thousand subscribing families spend an average of about three hours watching pay-TV out of better than thirty hours offered. We are not disappointed with that average. It proves that people will use pay-TV as purely supplemental to commercial TV. They will decide to pay for something they want to see in exactly the same way the family decides to go out for dinner, go to the theater, or a sports event.

"From our standpoint, as the largest nonnetwork broadcasting company in the country, we would be foolish to do anything to jeopardize the profit structure of commercial TV," Tom said. "We are convinced that pay-TV does not do that. It is simply an extra convenience of modern living. It is the only really feasible, economical way to bring the best of entertainment, and the biggest current sports event into the home, with no blackout areas. It is bound to come. The only question is when, and RKO General is staying in the field to make sure it has a head start when the real breakthrough does come."

Regardless of whether he relishes the role, Tom O'Neil will always be remembered for having co-starred with Howard Hughes in RKO Pictures' last thriller in 1955. This was not a movie, but a real-life drama which intrigued the American public and is regarded as one of the classic coups in American business.

The most important long-range result of the deal was that it unlocked for the first time the vaults of Hollywood's film libraries to TV. At the time this was an epochal achievement. What impressed the public was that Tom O'Neil paid $25 million for a few thousand spools of exposed celluloid. The deal was consummated in the cockpit of a Hughes Convair an hour out of Los Angeles, en route to Las Vegas. The two men shook hands on it, whereupon Hughes, who had been flying the plane, excused himself, left Tom at the controls for the first time in his life, and went to the men's room.

Events leading to the handshake were somewhat bizarre. They began with Tom's conviction that movies—lots of movies—were needed for successful TV programming, especially for a nonnetwork station. In 1953 he bought from the Bank of America the rights to thirty full-length features held as security for loans which hadn't paid out. He paid $1,350,000 for the right to show and rent to other TV stations around the country, but there were deadlines. Some features he could show for six months, others for a year. These thirty films were enough to prove the correctness of Tom's theory about the adaptability of movies to TV programming, but they did not long satisfy TV's voracious appetite. By early 1955 he needed more, and a financial friend tipped him that Howard Hughes might be induced to sell RKO's extensive film library if the price were high enough.

After some difficulty Tom persuaded another friend who knew Hughes to contact the RKO chief to inquire whether negotiations could be carried on. In a day or two Tom received a call from a representative of the quixotic, non-social multimillionaire, Howard Hughes—whom, incidentally Tom grew to like. The procedure Tom was to follow, if he wanted to see Hughes, was straight out of a late-TV movie. A car would pick up Tom at his home in Greenwich, Connecticut, and he was to have a bag packed for a week's trip. Yes, he could bring along Jack Poor, Vice-President and lawyer (later RKO General president), but no one else.

The next evening a big black sedan pulled up to Tom's door in Greenwich, with two men in it. Tom was driven to La Guardia and a second car picked up Jack Poor at his home. At the airport, a TWA sleeper plane was waiting for them, and within a few minutes of their boarding, the ramp was wheeled away and the plane took off. They were not told where the plane was going. They suspected it was to be a long flight because the berths were made up, and guessed it was Los Angeles.

This guess proved correct. Upon arrival, they were met

by a chauffeured car, driven to the Beverly Hills Hotel, and ushered in through a side entrance. Tom was told his name was Martin Wood. He was to be addressed by this name at all times and was asked to respond naturally to it in public. This was a disguise of dubious value because Tom is a highly visible individual and many of the hotel personnel knew him. Advance reservations had been made and Tom and Jack were ushered to the Hughes suite as soon as they arrived. There were daily meetings for a week, when Hughes suddenly suggested the night flight to Las Vegas. This took place on July 17 and, as related, the final handshake came an hour after the plane took off, while Jack Poor and Hughes' lawyer dozed in the back.

The purchase caused many heads to wag in disapproval, including those of a few General Tire directors. But W.O. was ebullient about it. "It's a great deal," he enthused. "That Tom, he makes money."

In the transaction General Teleradio, Inc., bought RKO Pictures from the sole owner, Howard Hughes. Included were two unreleased films, *The Conqueror* and *Jet Pilot,* both starring the then-top box-office attraction John Wayne. Hughes bought back these features for $8 million. The sale also included the cost of printing and advertising the films, which were to be distributed through RKO Teleradio's elaborate system of domestic and foreign film exchanges, which brought the projected, over-all price to $12 million.

This transaction was followed quickly by Tom's sale of the license to use RKO's film library—750 features and more than a thousand short subjects—for $12.2 million in cash and $3 million in two years, reserving to RKO Teleradio the TV rights in all five cities in which General had stations.

Tom also reserved the right for his new company, RKO

WM. M. O'NEIL,
*the oldest son, who is
not directly affiliated
with General Tire.*

T. F. O'NEIL,
*Chairman of the Board of
Directors, The General
Tire & Rubber Company.*

JOHN J. O'NEIL,
*Chairman of the Finance
Committee, The General
Tire & Rubber Company.*

M. G. O'NEIL,
*President of The
General Tire &
Rubber Company.*

TOP: *Research and development are important to General Tire's total operations.*

BOTTOM: *A huge dynamometer, capable of speeds up to 300 miles per hour, is used to test tires at the Brittain, Ohio, test center.*

General Tire's huge synthetic rubber manufacturing facility at Odessa, Texas, produces 40,000 long tons per year.

Diversity of products is reflected in these
scenes from General Tire's plants. TOP LEFT:
Tire-building is big business.
BOTTOM LEFT: *Nygen and fabric are processed*
at Barnesville, Georgia.
BELOW: *Tractor and trailer fully equipped with General tires.*
BOTTOM: *Giant earth-moving equipment moves tons*
of dirt and rock with the help of General tires.

Wrought iron and steel are produced at General Tire's
A. M. Beyers Company in Pittsburgh.

General Tire in the Space Age.
TOP: *The founding group of the Aerojet Engineering Corporation.*

BOTTOM: *Bill O'Neil and the distinguished astrophysicist, Dr. Theodore von Kármán, rocket expert and founder of Aerojet.*

*Gemini IV/Titan II launch vehicle in a
flawless liftoff at Cape Kennedy bears
Astronauts James McDivitt and Edward
White on their "walk in space" mission.
Both first- and second-stage propulsion
for Gemini flights are supplied by
Aerojet-General liquid-fuel engines.*

Teleradio, to 150 of the 750 feature films for eighteen months. He also secured first TV showing. There were other favorable concessions. The basic rights to the picture negatives for motion-picture-theater reissue were retained, as were the story rights, so that any of the 750 films could be remade at any time.

The skeptics were highly vocal when the $25-million transaction was announced. But within a short time RKO Teleradio had recovered its purchase money. After this it sold the RKO lot to Desilu Productions, created the Million Dollar Movie concept of programming, and its own stations profited immeasurably from the big film library.

When the Hughes deal was made, Tom was in charge of what had become a $35-million entertainment complex, including five wholly owned TV stations and the 569-affiliate Mutual Network. In number of stations it was the largest radio network, stretching from New England to the West Coast. Tom disposed of Mutual in 1957, certainly through no lack of faith in radio as an entertainment and advertising medium. He had too large a stake in radio for that. He sold Mutual because of the self-competition the network was beginning to create for RKO General's other expanding properties. The pattern of national radio advertising via network advertising had begun to change. Radio stations were finding local advertising more profitable.

Network advertising, which once commanded 60 per cent of all radio advertising, by 1957 accounted for only about 10 per cent. In the 1930s the top fifty stations in the United States were affiliated with either CBS or NBC. In 1964, only five major network-affiliated radio stations appeared among the top fifty. The rest were independents.

Tom points out, however, that radio continues to be big business because it produces results at low cost. He explains that there are forty million automobile radios alone, and that at least thirty-five million car owners may be reached on every average weekday. Eight-seven per cent of all new cars sold are radio-equipped.

As for RKO General's TV coverage, through its stations in five major markets, it blankets 30 per cent of the U.S. market. Tom inaugurated a strong national sales organization which sells advertising on all the stations as a "package." This form of merchandising has been highly successful and, of course, puts RKO General in direct competition with the major networks.

Like W.O.'s General Tire "proposition," Tom's advertising package has a salable difference from that of the major networks. For one thing, it has special advantages for national advertisers whose prime merchandising objective is to reach only the large metropolitan markets. RKO General stations also maintain alert sales departments in their local areas. They follow in the best tradition of General's local dealer; they are close to their customers' problems, and adhering to General's slogan "goes a long way to make friends."

No one yardstick can measure the success of RKO General. The complete story, like that of Aerojet-General alone, would require its own volume. The fact that RKO General has become the largest independent in the radio and television industry says much. So does the growth in sales and profits.

In 1947, when Tom O'Neil moved into the Yankee Network operation, sales were $2.5 million. In 1964, RKO General sales of $64 million yielded profits after taxes of $7 million. Of this, 80 per cent came from broadcasting revenue, an important fact to remember in connection with the probable future growth, in view of the ceiling on broadcasting stations and Tom's opinions about investing profits in other businesses, particularly nonmanufacturing and service enterprises.

In General Tire's Fiftieth Anniversary year, RKO General's other interests included the RKO Sound Studios in New York City for the filming of TV commercials and industrial films; the Musak background-music franchise for the Boston and Providence areas; the pay-TV experiment in Hartford; the theater and community antenna systems in the Southwest; the Pittsburgh Outdoor Advertising Corporation; and an interesting new subsidiary, Electronics Leasing Corporation of New York City. The latter has great expansion possibilities. Its primary business is leasing television sets to hospitals, hotels, and motels. A market is developing for leased color television sets in public places. This may also prove economical in the future for home rentals. This subsidiary also has the exclusive U.S. franchise for the "Teletracer," a Dutch invention for paging physicians, salesmen, and others. To be paged, all a person need do is to carry in his pocket a special low-key transistor radio. In 1965 RKO General purchased the controlling interest of Fleetwood Corporation, Canada's largest manufacturer of TV sets, radios, and home electronics equipment.

All these have substantial growth possibilities. Of special interest was RKO General's acquisition in 1964 of a controlling interest in Frontier Airlines. Frontier characterizes itself as "one of the nation's leading local-service airlines." Headquartered in Denver, it serves sixty-five cities in Colorado, Arizona, Missouri, Montana, Nebraska, North and South Dakota, Utah, and Wyoming. W.O. would be pleased that Kansas City is on its map. A number of places on its routes have growth rates among the highest in the United States. Frontier flies thirty-five planes, which are being converted to fifty-two-passenger

Convair 580s. And Frontier has already diversified. It owns a Denver firm which leases automobiles and rents mobile homes.

Tom had an interesting reply when asked why he was attracted to an airline which represents only a small percentage of the revenue miles flown in the United States.

"We feel," he said, "about the airlines today as we felt about TV back in 1947. We didn't invest in NBC or CBS; we bought a relatively small network and built it up according to our specifications." He pointed to a framed copy of General Tire's first advertisement which hangs on his office wall. "That paragraph applies," he said. " 'We have no old methods of our own to cling to through sentiment, stubbornness or economy. We have no past of our own to handicap us, and we do have the pasts and the presents of others to warn us of pitfalls.' "

Tom is a businessman in the best O'Neil tradition. He is much like his father in affability, self-reliance, and what might be called economic creativity. He has one habit which goes back, in an odd way, over two generations. Michael carried in his vest pocket a pair of small scissors, rounded at the points, such as dealers in dry goods used to snip swatches from yard goods. Michael continued to carry the scissors long after he ceased to be a dry-goods or department-store owner. He used them to clip newspaper items which interested him. In later years, these included business failures which he left on W.O.'s desk. Tom carries no draper's scissors, but he has an equally distinctive and ever-present pocket-piece—a slide rule. He uses it during a conversation with amazing speed, precision, and a total lack of concentration. There appears to be an ancestral link between this vocational attachment to the draper's scissors and the slide rule.

16

"Anything legal, moral, and tax-free"

$\mathbf{B}$ILL O'NEIL left an imprint as distinctive as any tire tread on all the new roads General has traveled, especially after World War II.

Even in what is generally regarded as the highly conventionalized field of pension funding he took a creative approach suggested in 1946 by his son John, back from the war. John became the financial troubleshooter for the company in Akron, and his father's around-the-clock top assistant. Win Fouse was approaching seventy and wanted to step down as active treasurer and chief financial officer. This he did, at a meeting of the board of directors in January 1948, at which time John was elected to succeed him.

John was the bachelor son and lived at home. He was his father's sounding board and confidant during and after normal working hours—the kind of individual W.O. needed at his side. Their long discussions, especially about financial matters, laid the basis for John's career as the financial architect and planner for the company.

John graduated from Holy Cross in 1938, at the same

commencement at which W.O. received an honorary Doctor of Laws degree. This caused W.O. to tell people occasionally, especially if they didn't know him well, that "John and I graduated from college together." If he was rewarded with a puzzled look, he was pleased. He never explained his little joke. John went on to earn a law degree at Harvard. W.O. professed to have a low opinion of lawyers, but he was as proud of John's degree as any father would be, and occasionally took delight in pointing out that he outranked John scholastically in the subject because of his honorary doctorate.

Almost as soon as he returned from military service and began to function as W.O.'s liaison man in many areas, John became aware of the great interest in a pension plan that was developing among the salaried workers. General had no such program, so John brought the subject to W.O.'s attention. There is no question that W.O. knew about the interest in the pension plan, but for all his seeming impulsiveness at times, he could also procrastinate until his attention was fixed on a subject, and especially until his imagination was fired by a "different" idea—a creative approach. He had no herd instinct, no liking at all for running with the pack. If there was a different way of doing a thing, W.O. could be depended upon to become interested. Otherwise the proposition generated nothing but inertia in him. But if a "different idea" put the emphasis on individualism, or permitted General Tire know-how to be used creatively, his inertia became momentum. He had built his tire business on the premise that "if everybody is doing a certain thing one way, there is probably a better way to do it and charge more money for it." His individualism in radio was already beginning to pay off—television would become profitable within two or three years. His approach to the exotic field of rocketry was unconventional, and his method of operating in the international field was not in any book.

W.O.'s 1936 decision to establish a mechanical rubber goods division was not the staid conventional diversification of other rubber companies. General's first mechanical rubber goods plant was located at Wabash, Indiana. From it, both before and after the war, developed the Industrial Products Division, first under Howard Dodge and later under O. A. Vinnedge, who was elected a General Tire director in 1957. In General's Fiftieth Anniversary year, the headquarters of the Division remained in Wabash, Indiana, with other plants at Logansport and Evansville, both in Indiana. These facilities have grown to produce a bewildering assortment of metal, rubber, and extruded flexible and rigid plastic component parts for the automotive, aircraft, furniture, electric appliance, and communications industries, and for the military.

The usual rubber company's mechanical rubber goods division made belting, brake linings, battery boxes, and other staples. To get involved in transportation, home furnishings, appliances, and communications requires a different concept, a creative approach, plenty of money spent on research, and the willingness to make an imaginative philosophy a corporate way of life.

The mechanical rubber goods division, as it was originally known, was well along before the phrase *population explosion* became current, but even then it will be noted that W.O.'s brainchildren came to have large families. They all "exploded" rather than gestated progeny by sedate planned-parenthood techniques. The success of the Chemical/Plastics Division, RKO General, Aerojet-General, and General Tire International are all proof of this. They have proliferated far beyond their original bounds. The success General's diversified divisions have had in themselves diversifying has been responsible for making the parent company's over-all reputation unique in American industry.

W.O.'s philosophy toward expansion into new fields was based on two great faiths—faith in the private-enterprise way of accomplishment and faith in the capabilities of General Tire people. He revealed this trait clearly by responding to John's urgings to set up a pension fund in 1947. For all his display of iconoclasm, W.O. was conservative and conventional in many respects. His first approach to the pension problem was to assign John to study the various insurance company plans available.

There are many good ones, of course, and John studied them carefully. He learned that probably less than 1 per cent of all companies direct their own pension-fund investments. Most such projects are handled by an insurance company or by a bank. After six months, John reported his findings to his father. Both were concerned by the question of what would happen if they chose the insurance company's plan and changed their minds later. All the money paid in—and a little bit more—would come back, but not in individual benefits large enough to be meaningful. John was eager to handle the company fund, but he did not press his point of view until W.O. showed no enthusiasm for any of the standard plans. They sounded a great deal alike to him, too conventional. He would have preferred to invest "a million dollars or two the way we want to do it."

Then John remarked, "Of course, if we handled our own funds, the profits would be tax-free as long as they remain in the pension fund and are not used to help the company in any way."

That did it. W.O. was for anything that was moral, legal, and tax-free. He spent a long moment or two, leaning back in his chair, studying the ceiling of his office, a characteristic way he had of concentrating deeply. Finally he spoke. "You mean we can make deals and whatever the profits are, we don't have to pay taxes on them?"

"Certainly," John answered, repeating the necessity for keeping the profits in the pension fund. W.O. was not discouraged by that. Just so he didn't have to pay them out in taxes.

After that W.O.'s decision came quickly. "I think we can take a million dollars or two and pick up enough little deals to make it worthwhile. Let's start out on our own. Then, as you point out, if we want to go into an insurance company's plan later, we can. It would be easier to do that than the other way around."

That was the decision in 1947. There is no question that the tax-free feature was decisive. Also, W.O. loved to make "deals," so the combination of being able to indulge his pleasure and take a tax-free return was like giving a small boy a pass to an amusement park. It was probably true, too, that W.O. did not quite realize how large the fund would become over the years, with all salaried and hourly employees of General Tire, Aerojet-General, RKO General, and A. M. Byers covered.

W.O.'s fondness for making deals was well known. He was constantly bombarded by propositions in many fields, ranging from automatic washing machines to airplane parts, and from buyouts to the offer of technical-service fees for supplying General Tire know-how, much as was done under the International plan. Someone at General at the time, paraphrasing Emerson, said, "A good idea will beat a path to W.O.'s door."

The first "little deal" that started the General Pension Fund was originally presented to W.O. as a possible diversification for the company itself. It was a Cleveland company. Its head and major stockholder, who wanted to sell it for $7 million, was a friend of W.O. He remained so, despite the fact that conversations were fruitless over several months. They occurred two or three times a week in W.O.'s office. Apparently W.O. would talk about everything else but the matter at hand. This was typical of W.O. in certain moods and under certain circumstances; his son Tom once said of this trait, "If you put Job and W.O. in the same tent to reach a decision, Job would be the first to come out screaming in frustration."

Finally the owner found a Boston buyer for his manufacturing business. And when the purchaser—a pension fund, incidentally—completed the conventional financing with a $3-million bank loan added to its own $3 million in cash, it needed an additional $1,050,000.

This was the type of "little deal" that interested W.O. General's pension fund supplied the $1,050,000, taking title to the land and building and leasing them back to the new company with the rental keyed to sales. Sales boomed. Within three and a half years, $1.5 million in rent was collected, for a profit at the end of that time of $450,000.

This was the pension fund's first transaction and is still in effect. It was negotiated by John and George Smith, of whom more later. John refers to an investment of this kind as a "three-leg" deal. It is secured by the intrinsic value of the property; the lease; and the third reassuring "leg"— that General could use the property as a warehouse if this should become necessary. Common stock, for instance in General Motors, is a "one-leg" deal, pegged to the single factor of the stock's market value. A "two-leg" deal would consist of buying property and leasing it to General Motors, the rental price keyed to sales. Here the value of the property and value of the lease would be two protecting factors. If General had a potential use for the property, the deal would, of course, become a "three-legger."

Toward the end of 1949, John decided to settle once and for all a question which had been in his mind for a long time—whether he had a vocation to the priesthood. He entered the seminary in early 1950 and remained through 1953, returning to the company in 1954 after establishing *The Pope Speaks,* a quarterly which is the only English publication containing all the Pope's current important statements. This publication preceded by several years the ecumenical movement and the widespread use of English, instead of Latin, in Roman Catholic Church usage. As a sideline John continues to head the publication, which has widespread circulation among the clergy and laity of both Christians and Jews, and is recognized as a major instrument for interfaith understanding.

John, who is the chief financial officer of General Tire and its financial architect, functions under the title of Chairman Finance Committee. He devotes most of his time to major financial policy and to the direction of the investments which have grown out of the original pension fund. The modern General Investment Funds, of which John is Chairman-President, consist of "Pension, Profit-Sharing, Charitable and Other Investment Funds."

By 1965 the total assets of these funds were well over $150 million. This included some $100 million in the various pension funds covering the General Tire, Aerojet-General, RKO General, and A. M. Byers Company employees; more than $40 million in the Profit-Sharing Fund and the equity funds for the employees; the balance is in charitable foundations and certain other investment funds. Approximately 50,000 employees were covered in 1965. At their present level, General's Pension Funds assure a high degree of security, and benefits have been improved several times.

The investment portfolio is widely diversified. Holdings range from government and corporate bonds through most other types of readily marketable securities—many with a convertible flavor. Always the emphasis is "protect against both inflation and deflation." John refers to a major purchase of common stock in a company as "instant diversification." At any given time he presides over some two hundred investments, including common stock in well over a hundred companies in perhaps fifty major industries.

In view of W.O.'s well-known belief in the stock market as necessary to the well-being of the economic system, he would look with pride and approval on this portfolio. The emphasis placed on industries "faced to the future" would not escape him. There is special interest, too, in mortgage loan and real estate holdings. In 1965 these were well over $25 million. Most of the real estate investments include a rental arrangement based on sales or profit—the inflation hedge. These have been profitable, and perhaps best represent what W.O. had in mind when he referred to "the little deals we can pick up" when he gave John a go-ahead with the first Cleveland deal in 1948.

John directs the General Investment Funds operation from his headquarters in Washington, D.C., where the funds have major real estate holdings. The location is convenient to Akron, New York City, and Pittsburgh, the headquarters of the A. M. Byers Company, a General subsidiary with an investment sideline. This century-old, world's largest wrought-iron pipe producer, in which General acquired a majority interest in 1956, has since diversified into steel pipe and flat rolled products. With the purchase of the Galis Manufacturing Company of Fairmont, West Virginia, it diversified into the manufacturing of mining and material-handling machinery. In 1965 the Missouri Steel Castings Co. and the Missouri Rogers Company, manufacturers of rock-crushing equipment much in demand by the nation's superhighway building programs, were purchased. Byers also has a real estate operation and its own investment portfolio—the "instant diversification" medium so much needed when it was a one-product company. Byers has played a unique role in the parent company by proving an excellent testing ground for executive personnel. Sam Salem, who was general manager of Byers, is President of General's Chemical/Plastics Division, and Wendell J. Gurtner, who was in Byers' treasury department after twenty years of service at General's Wabash operations became General's Treasurer in 1965.

With the assistance of a relatively small staff, John administers all details of the Investment Funds and all moneys are held in trust by banks. Since the assets are for the most part not corporate assets, the General Investment Funds cannot be considered an example of General Tire diversification. But in a sense it is the most spectacularly diversified of all General Tire activities, and the least publicized.

John makes his home in Washington with his wife, the former Helene Connellan. They were married in 1959 and have four children: Helene, John James, Jr., Ann, and Jane.

17

The Fabulous Fifties
and a patent suit

THE 1950s were fabulous for General Tire. Sales, which had totaled $92.5 million in 1949, zoomed to $677 million in 1959. Profits, after taxes, which averaged a little more than $2.5 million a year in the 1940s, soared to a $10-million average during the years of the 1950s. The company's earned surplus in 1949 was about $24 million, in 1959 more than $66 million. The common stock was split two for one in 1952 and three for one in 1957.

Tire sales—both passenger-car and truck—outgrew the capacity of the company's two plants at Akron and Waco, Texas, requiring the addition of a third plant at Mayfield, Kentucky. Sparking the growth was a cascading stream of basic research discoveries and revolutionary improvements in tire-production techniques. The changeover to the "chemical tire," to take the place of the prewar natural-rubber-and-cotton variety, was almost complete.

It seems that W.O. never had just a single reason for his moves. And in the case of his willingness to plow back millions of dollars into chemical research—in rubber, cord fibers, and other areas—he had at least three. One was his faith in the future of synthetic rubber; particularly in the ability of scientists to develop various kinds, each with specific advantages for different purposes. Another was his desire to add value to the technical services General provided to its international affiliates which, as we have seen, began to proliferate in 1946. There is no question that a third motivation was a desire to be free from worries in connection with the wide price swings which plagued the natural rubber and cotton markets. He had lived with these ever since 1915 and was a recognized buying authority, but he did not like being dependent on natural rubber sources half the world away and on the vagaries of the cotton market. While others invested in rubber plantations in the Far East and in Africa, W.O. invested domestically in research as soon as the "chemical tire" became a dot on the horizon.

General's "Fabulous Fifties" started off promptly in 1950 with important happenings in Tom's radio-TV operation, as well as at Aerojet and in Akron.

The Don Lee Network of forty-five stations on the West Coast was purchased—the first major step in General's climb from being a small regional network in New England to its eventual role as the country's largest independent radio and TV operation.

At Aerojet, in 1950 the parent company provided the financing and management skills needed to build and operate what has become the Free World's largest research and development, testing, and production center for solid, liquid, and nuclear-propulsion systems. It is located on 23,000 acres near Sacramento, California. In the mid-1960s this was only one of a dozen Aerojet-General facilities, in California, Florida, Maryland, New York, and Arkansas, but it is the largest in number of personnel and is where important work has been done on practically every U.S. space-age program.

At Akron in 1949, a discovery was made in General's five-year-old research laboratory which shook the rubber world and touched off a legal battle over General's U.S. Patent Number 2,964,083, the reverberations of which will continue, probably, for years.

From this point, the best way to bring the multilateral activities of the 1950s into perspective is to summarize the decade year by year. This will at least give a panoramic view and show why business writers began to be so fascinated by General Tire's amazingly diversified growth, a phenomenon which is still continuing:

1950 — Oil-extended rubber announced by General at Akron.

1950 — Don Lee Network on West Coast purchased.

1950 — Sacramento plant of Aerojet-General built.

1950 — Vinyl plastic production begun at Jeannette, Pennsylvania.

1950 — Chemical Division started.

1952 — General Teleradio (now RKO General) bought New York's Stations WOR-AM and TV.

1953 — Pennsylvania Athletic Products Division expanded.

1953 — Nygen Cord fabric for tires perfected.

1953 — Further expansion in production of chemicals, foam rubber, and rigid plastics.

1953 — Ground broken for $6-million plant to produce PVC resin (basis of vinyl plastic) in Ashtabula, Ohio.

1954 — Ashtabula PVC plant opened with capacity of 25 million pounds of resin annually; since trebled to 75 million pounds.

1954 — General becomes world's largest producer of vinyl film and sheeting with purchase of Bolta Products, Lawrence, Massachusetts, and Textileather, Toledo, Ohio, for $10 million in General preferred stock.

1955 – RKO Pictures bought from Howard Hughes for $25 million, a milestone in TV history.

1955 – Long-term lease signed with El Paso Natural Gas Company for Butadiene and Styrene to be piped to a new General synthetic rubber plant in Odessa, Texas. First synthetic plant built since the war; first by private enterprise (not a wartime plant bought from the government), ultramodern and completely instrumented.

1957 – General's Odessa rubber plant completed with capacity of 40,000 long tons a year; production later stepped up to 75,000 long tons.

1957 – Urethane foam (Polyfoam) developed as lightweight cushioning material for myriad uses in furniture, automobiles, aviation, insulation applications, and mattresses.

1958 – A. M. Byers Company, century-old wrought-iron pipe manufacturer purchased and diversification program begun.

1959 – Construction of a major new tire plant begun at Mayfield, Kentucky, General's third domestic tire plant.

And so it went. This list is by no means complete, and to make it so would defeat the purpose of giving a bird's-eye view of the diversification which occurred in the ten-year period.

On August 21, 1950, W.O. reached his sixty-fifth birthday. Like most persons of Irish ancestry, he seldom mentioned age and it is doubtful if many besides his oldest and closest associates knew exactly how old he was. It is safe to assume none of them suggested an office party with sixty-five candles on it.

W.O. had not been really robust since the early thirties, when a broken ankle was followed by a blood clot in his leg; only a very advanced type of treatment is credited with saving his life. After that, he had occasional attacks of phlebitis, which made walking painful and difficult. Nevertheless, at sixty-five he was energetic and forceful in his movements and business activities. Not many knew the extent of his health problems. More knew that his mother was still alive and active, and this augured well for his longevity.

By 1950, W.O. had more zest than ever for business. He made plans for the long future as enthusiastically and confidently as when he was thirty and starting General Tire.

As soon as the war ended, General's new research laboratory was added to the Akron complex. It was there that the discovery was made that "shook the rubber world" and proved to be one of the most valuable advances in the history of synthetic rubber—this is what makes it one of the truly epochal achievements of General's Fabulous Fifties.

The discovery, commonly referred to as "oil-extended rubber," was made by three scientists working in General's Akron laboratory. They were Gilbert Swart, the expert W.O. had summoned to Aerojet to check out his hunch about the relationship of rocket-propellant chemistry to rubber chemistry; Emert S. Pfau; and the late Kermit V. Weinstock. What these three did was to add an inordinate amount of oil to a batch of high Mooney Styrene-Butadiene rubber, which is an extremely tough and difficult synthetic to work with. The three scientists have since testified that they did this in order to make the high Mooney as pliant as possible, and perhaps produce a low-grade rubber suitable for floor mats. To their amazement, the mixture produced an excellent type of tread rubber, equal if not superior to the GR-S synthetic then being produced in the government-owned synthetic-rubber plants.

As it turned out, the discovery meant that enough low-cost oil could be substituted for expensive high Mooney to produce a rubber suitable for use as a high-quality tread stock material. This tough oil-extended synthetic could be sold five cents per pound below the market price for standard GR-S because the end-product yield was increased by that much.

General's patent application on "oil-extended rubber" was filed on November 20, 1950, setting up a whole series of strange events. On December 10, 1954, a little more than four years later, and at a time when the industry had adapted the process and was producing "oil-extended rubber" with the savings and advantages cited in General's patent application, the Company was officially informed that the patent would be issued on payment of a fee of $30, plus one dollar for each separate claim for the invention over twenty. General had originally filed for thirty claims, but compromised on the twenty-two granted.

Just thirty-two days after General was notified that its patent would be granted, the Company was informed that approval had been withdrawn; the application was taken from the Patent Office examiner who had devoted more than four years to it and given to another. The second examiner took far less time than had the first. Just four months after the case was transferred to him, he rejected it *in toto* on April 15, 1955.

This turn of events left General two forms of appeal. It could appeal to the Court of Customs and Patent Appeals —the usual procedure—or it could appeal to the U.S. District Court, in which case not only would the Patent Office records be reviewed but new evidence and the testimony of witnesses could also be heard.

After the alternative routes were discussed with W.O., the decision was made to sue in the U.S. District Court in the District of Columbia. W.O. wanted a complete airing.

The Patent Office was the defendant, of course, and

General Tire the plaintiff. Ordinarily, in such cases, the Patent Office is represented by an Assistant Solicitor who prepares his case from evidence supplied to him by the Patent Office, and it is generally conceded that the Patent Office benefits from some presumption of objectivity and accumulated experience.

Surprisingly, for the first time in the history of patent applications, the U.S. Department of Justice entered the case, with one of its lawyers assisting in the defense. Who applied the pressure to bring the Department of Justice into the case—whether someone in the government or in the rubber industry—will always be open to conjecture.

At any rate, General won the suit. On December 13, 1960, six months after the trial and ten years after filing its original application, General Tire was granted U.S. Patent 2,964,083.

After its patent was granted, General requested a royalty of three eighths of a cent a pound from competitors using the process. This would amount to a very small proportion of the savings to the rubber industry by utilizing General's invention. It is estimated that the industry as a whole saves approximately $135 million per year in the utilization of this invention.

Some of the smaller companies recognized General's patent and accepted the licensing agreement, but none of the major competitors felt bound by the patent. General filed suit against Goodyear * and U.S. Rubber in the U.S. District Court in Cleveland, and was about to sue the others when Firestone succeeded in getting a countersuit on the docket of the Federal Court in Baltimore, contending that General was a party to the wartime rubber pool

* In February, 1966, General and Goodyear reached an out-of-court settlement involving this patent. Under the terms of the settlement, Goodyear was granted a nonexclusive license for use of the invention, and General dismissed this patent-infringement lawsuit against the company.

[206]

and therefore that all companies had a right to help themselves to the General discovery. The suit asked that General be stopped from exercising its royalty claim—in other words, renounce its hard-won U.S. Patent 2,964,083.

Rubber World (October 1964) characterized this as "perhaps the largest [patent suit] in the history of the United States. . . . Practically every large rubber company in the world is involved one way or another. . . . The case is being watched by observers from [many foreign countries] and litigation in all these various places is pending. . . . Estimates of the number of documents introduced and to be introduced in testimony, pro and con, range from 50,000 to 80,000. . . . The number of lawyers involved is conjectural, because all the corporations, companies and groups that have retained legal assistance cannot be known. . . . A deliberately modest estimate might be fifty. . . . The newspapers seem dimly aware that something is going on. . . . The lawyers, of course, refuse to discuss any of the details of the case while it is in progress: ethics. . . . Steps remaining would be for the loser in Baltimore to carry the case to the Federal Court of Appeals . . . beyond that lies the Supreme Court of the United States, which may or may not consider the matter. . . . These two final steps, of course, lie years ahead in the unforeseeable future."

General Tire bought the Pennsylvania Rubber Company of Jeannette, Pennsylvania, in 1945. It was one of the oldest tire companies in the industry, and those whose memory goes back to the 1920s still remembered its famous Vacuum Cup tread, which set up a distinctive whistling noise on pavements—a disadvantage which somehow became a status symbol in its day. Pennsylvania capitalized on it by advertising it as "the sound of safety."

When General purchased it, the company still made

tires, but the end of its business which W.O. felt was "faced to the future" was its Athletic Goods Division; he foresaw that athletics and sports would boom in the postwar period. When the purchase of Pennsylvania was news, W.O. never failed to tell anyone who spoke to him about it, "You know, Pennsylvania makes sixty-five per cent of all the tennis balls in the country." He gave the distinct impression of being a great tennis enthusiast, especially after he learned that the number of tennis courts in public parks was declining. He developed a strong sense of indignation over the fact that many were being eliminated in favor of softball diamonds and outdoor basketball courts. This discrimination became academic, however, after Pennsylvania developed a full line of rubber-covered softballs and basketballs, as well as footballs, water-balls, and balls of all kinds that traditionally had been leather-covered. In time, the Pennsylvania rubber-covered equivalents came to be officially approved for most scheduled scholastic and tournament play.

Without doubt the most exotic product Pennsylvania made in its Athletic Goods Division was an "official" badminton bird. The feathers—and just certain ones—from the right wing of a particular breed of goose which in France produces *pâté de foie gras* had to be used. W.O. took a dim view of this badminton bird from the start, and very soon its "feathers" were made of General rigid plastic.

It soon became apparent that W.O. had another use in mind for the Pennsylvania production facilities, as well as its expanding athletic-goods line. Somehow he had become interested in vinyl plastic, which was new, and had ascertained that, like rocket propellants, it could be produced by the same type of mills and calenders used in a rubber plant. He sold off the tire end of the Pennsylvania business, expanded the athletic-goods facilities, and began to produce vinyl film and sheeting. Firms known as "converters" sprang up all over the country. They bought the film in huge rolls, much as a newspaper buys newsprint, and their business was to print colorful patterns on the film to make it suitable for shower curtains, patterned tablecloths, "chintz" curtains, and many other household uses. The converter business lasted only a few years. Shipping costs made this middleman operation uneconomic, and the manufacturer took over the printing operation.

The vinyl sheeting—basically, just a thicker version of the film—came in solid colors and very early began to be embossed to produce a variety of leatherlike appearances. It was used mostly as furniture upholstery, especially for dinette sets. It was some time before it achieved living-room status, except for "contour chairs," which became as popular as hoola hoops.

Despite the newness of the art of producing vinyl film and sheeting, the operation at Jeannette was a success almost from the start. It was a complicated changeover from the tire-production facilities, but Jerry O'Neil and John E. Powers, a vice-president and company director, presided over it with marked success.

Then the company decision was made to erect at Ashtabula, Ohio, its own facility for the production of polyvinyl chloride resin (PVC), the basis of vinyl plastic. Several large chemical companies were already in the production of PVC, but because of its newness, the price was still high. Jerry believed that the normal competitive forces would soon bring down the price, and that General could profit most from using its PVC in its own end products, rather than by selling the chemical to other manufacturers. The trouble with this was that the Jeannette facility was not large enough to use an appreciable amount of the 25 million pounds of PVC which the $6-million

Ashtabula plant was scheduled to start pouring out in its first year. Jerry began to campaign for larger end-product facilities.

W.O. was enthusiastic about the idea because of the immediate success of the Jeannette operation, and assigned George Smith, a member of his staff who had found other diversifications in the past, to the project. (Smith, it will be remembered, was helpful in the first Investment Funds deal with John O'Neil.) W.O. called him a "bird-dog."

"George can pick up the scent of more deals than anyone I know," W.O. once said.

The deal he pursued in the vinyl field involved the two leaders of the then-fledgling industry. John Powers told W.O. and Jerry that Bolta Products of Lawrence, Massachusetts, could be purchased, and Smith found that Textileather of Toledo, Ohio, was likewise available. Both were relatively old established companies. Textileather had started out in 1911 making a leatherette cover for a nickel baseball, and Bolta in the 1920s, making hard-rubber pocket combs which also sold for a nickel. Both had expanded tremendously since the advent of the new vinyl plastics. Bolta—with a furniture upholstery called Bolta-flex—was the leader in that field, and Textileather was beginning to make inroads on the automotive market in nearby Detroit. The widespread adoption of vinyl car upholstery and interiors came just a few years later and has been a major factor in vinyl sales.

W.O. entered into negotiations for the two firms so enthusiastically—probably intending at first to buy one or the other—that he wound up acquiring both leaders in the field by an exchange of General Tire preferred stock. The acquisition made General the world's largest producer of vinyl film and sheeting—an industry "faced to the future" if ever there was one. This was great for General's pride of status, but of more practical advantage was the fact that with the Pennsylvania, Textileather, and Bolta plants, General's output of vinyl products was now large enough not only to make the Ashtabula PVC operation successful, but also to make trebling the output necessary in the next few years.

Very soon after the Ashtabula PVC plant went into production, its resin began to maintain a remarkable uniformity, a most desirable characteristic and one which troubled most PVC producers. Much of the credit went to Dr. A. L. Antonio, on loan from Aerojet-General, where he was in charge of solid-rocket developments and chemical activity. This was a typical case of a General Tire expert in one field helping solve the problems of another General Tire division. To this day, there is a good deal of this intra-company use of expert knowledge and ability. The team is the Big G, and from time to time you are expected to play different positions if you have a special or timely talent.

General plastics were soon being turned out in all forms from injection-molded cafeteria trays—and a plastic-raffia "bun basket" which for some reason became as common as salt shakers on restaurant tables—to glove-soft automotive upholstery. The big swing to vinyl car interiors had started. The trend has never stopped, as each year new and more beautiful vinyl fabrics are developed—some all-vinyl, some vinyl in combination with nylon and other synthetic fibers. General produces them all.

In fact, vinyl sheeting—whether used for car interiors, luggage, or handbags—has become a sophisticated product. It can be intricately embossed so as to be practically indistinguishable from ostrichskin, pigskin, alligator hide, or whatever the customer desires. Not for a long time have finishes been limited to a leatherlike appearance. Some of the new furniture and automobile upholstery can be made to look and feel like almost any rich fabric you care to name.

The technical limitations which, in the beginning, caused practically all vinyl sheeting to look like leather aroused the ire of the Leather Institute of America, especially if there was any comparison with leather made in the advertising. W.O. had a strong opinion about this, too. He came to regard leather as a "synthetic plastic." Any advertising the Leather Institute did to discredit plastic—and it began to do a good deal—angered him. He instructed his advertising people and sales department never to mention leather or to use any terms suggesting it. His opinion was that "leather is not in the same class with our vinyl." The leather people became most agitated when a "breathable" vinyl was developed which quickly became popular in the shoe industry. This was one stronghold leather meant to keep. To a large extent it has, but tremendous tonnages of vinyl are also used now for shoes, as well as large quantities of General's foam rubber for innersoles.

W.O.'s refusal in the early 1950s to introduce a passenger-car tire made of nylon as soon as most manufacturers did was a traumatic experience for Jerry, who bore the brunt of the organization's complaints about the delay. W.O. was impressed by the strength of nylon fabric—General had been making some aviation and truck tires of it for years—but the "stretch" which made nylon ideal for women's hose made it susceptible to developing "flat spots" when the car was parked in the garage overnight. The tires quickly returned to round after a few blocks of travel in the morning, but the temporary thump-thump-thump was disconcerting to premium-tire buyers who expected "extra comfort." W.O. also objected to the fact that every manufacturer would soon have a premium-priced tire made of nylon and General would have no distinctive advantage. There was also the technical problem of finding a satisfactory adhesive to bond the synthetic-rubber tread to the nylon carcass. The company's new chemical facility, started at Mogadore, near Akron, in 1950, another of Jerry's particular prides, came up with the adhesive Gen-Tac, which is still being sold to other manufacturers. The stretch problem was alleviated, and a tendency to tread cracking was solved, mostly by a sophisticated new production technique called "post-inflation curing." Everyone thought General was ready to roll out a nylon tire at last, and it was about time.

Nothing was further from W.O.'s mind. He saw no point in advertising Mr. Du Pont's nylon, something every other tire manufacturer had or could buy. The fact that Du Pont had spent millions advertising nylon, and that it had almost mystical acceptance as the first of the "miracle fibers," meant nothing to him compared with the exclusiveness of a product "with a difference." General developed its own special "dip" for further treating the processed nylon, and then W.O. insisted that General's cord be called Nygen, a combination of the words *nylon* and *General*. Nygen was extensively advertised as "pound for pound, stronger than steel cables," which it was, and the name *nylon* has never been applied to a premium General Tire.

At the time all this was going on, W.O.'s closest associates were almost unanimous in believing that he was wrong in not getting on the nylon bandwagon. Especially during the long months when competition was capitalizing on the newness of it, and before Nygen and Gen-Tac could be perfected. Of course they expressed this opinion to him many times. "It is tradition at General," *Fortune* magazine said once, "that it is O. K. to tell the boss he is haywire." Sometimes he would listen and the next morning reverse his field. But this time he didn't, happily, because every maker came to have nylon tires, but only General has Nygen.

And "the least of the difference is the difference in price."

18

The start of the
billion-dollar years

WHEN M. G. (Jerry) O'Neil was elected
President of The General Tire & Rubber Company at the
age of thirty-eight he remarked, "I've been in the tire business for thirty-eight years." And one's mind goes back to
the conversation W.O. had with a friend many years before, when he said: "I learned about business from hearing
my father talk about it at home. I would like my sons to do
the same thing. I think it is up to me to carry on the family tradition and do what my father did—teach them about
business while they are young."

Jerry was the youngest president of an Akron tire company when he was elected in 1960, but at that he was
eight years older than his father had been when he
founded General Tire. The timing of Jerry's election was
dictated by W.O.'s declining health. His mind, alert as
ever, was preoccupied most of the time with the future,
but in early 1960, W.O. was physically tired.

At the annual meeting of the board in the spring, W.O.
resigned as President but remained Chairman of the

Board. Jerry, who had been W.O.'s round-the-clock Executive Assistant in Akron for ten years, was his natural successor as President. He had been in on all the details of the oil-extended rubber discovery and the subsequent controversy from the beginning. He had directed the planning and start-up of the Odessa synthetic-rubber complex in 1957. The creation of the original Chemical Division was made his particular responsibility as early as 1951, and the new PVC plant at Ashtabula a little later. He saw the Plastics Division grow from the first handful of resin produced there to become the world's largest source for vinyl film and sheeting. Finished products ranged from golf bags to interiors for practically every make of automobile.

Nygen Cord was developed—with W.O. at his stubborn best about not calling it nylon—during Jerry's era as Executive Assistant to the President. And so were most of the chemical specialties such as Gen-Tac and important latices for the paint, paper, and textile industries.

Jerry was in on the beginning of the foam and reinforced plastics developments and, from the start of Aerojet-General's big jump into aerospace, he was the responsible Akron head for these bewildering activities. He had a prominent part in the development of the International affiliates program and, in fact, got his first experience with the company, after his graduation from college, in the Inter-Plant Division, which was responsible for coordinating the technical and production facilities of the various International affiliates. He spent several months with the Venezuelan affiliate in 1949 before returning to Akron.

Jerry would have been graduated from Holy Cross in 1943 but for the outbreak of the war. He was in the middle of his senior year when he left to join the Army Air Corps. This meant that he still had a semester to finish for his degree, which he did after returning from the service in the fall of 1945. He was graduated in February 1946.

W.O.'s last great business enthusiasm was for the patent covering General's discovery of oil-extended rubber. The decision of the Federal District Court in Washington, ordering the Patent Office to issue the patent to General as originally granted before the strange reversal, was delivered orally June 10, 1960.

W.O. was informed of the favorable decision at his home by a phone call from Washington from the Company's Chief Patent Attorney, Frank Earnheart. It was probably the last great bit of good business news that W.O. heard in his lifetime. He was already desperately ill, but the news visibly cheered him. He felt that an American principle had been vindicated—the American system of patents, with the right of a patentee to license others who want to use an original discovery, had been upheld. He felt justified in having done his part to uphold it against the foreign principle and spirit of "corporate collectivism," as exemplified by the wartime pooling practices of the industry. And high time, he thought. The war had been over fifteen years. Anyone who had an ideological justification for "the pool" during the emergency of wartime could hardly hold it with common sense nearly a generation after the emergency.

W.O. did not live to see the actual issuance of the patent on December 13, 1960. His death came on September 4, in Akron.

Tom O'Neil was elected Chairman of the Board at its meeting on April 4, 1961. Tom had a detailed knowledge of the business dating back to his first days with the company as a tire salesman on the West Coast, plus his experience as Washington manager and store manager in Boston, before beginning his spectacular success with the radio and TV properties of General, building up to the creation of RKO General in 1959 and the remarkable diversifications of that end of the business into pay-TV, community antenna services, an airline, a Canadian television manufacturing company, and all the rest.

Tom has been committed to living in New York for many years now because the radio and television interests, as well as several other of General's diversifications center there.

John is the son whose business interest is instinctively financial. He is an idealist—and a philosopher much as his father was in certain moods—but his attitude toward business reminds one of a chessplayer's. He has a good deal of scholastic philosophy in his educational background, and he thinks in syllogisms. He trusts the logic of his conclusions if his major and minor premises are right. This is not to make him appear pedantic, which he decidedly is not, but he is a born financial strategist, and some of his best planning, both for the company and for the Investment Funds, has been based on pure logic.

All three of W.O.'s sons in the company inherited W.O.'s imagination, enthusiasm for business, and an impatience with the *status quo*. All are expansion-minded when "all the factors check out."

"All the brothers are interested in the over-all picture," Jerry once told a newspaperman who was trying to clarify their respective positions in the corporate structure. This is of course true, but it is equally true—and quite remarkable—that each has come to his area of specific responsibility naturally, and that the company has gained by what W.O. always loved to call "General Tire know-how"—in this case, in the best use of the specific talents of the three sons of Will and Grace O'Neil, Tom, John, and Jerry.

Tom and Jerry are the wits of the family. If this seems to leave John out it may be because, as Tom says, "There's nothing funny about money." All three are licensed pilots, with Tom and Jerry the most enthusiastic about flying. Tom learned sometime after being left alone at the controls of Howard Hughes' plane over the Nevada flatlands; Jerry learned to fly before the war and was a flying instructor in the service. All three are low-handicap golfers. John amiably concedes that Tom and Jerry are the better flyers, but just as amiably lays claim to the family golf championship.

Of all four of the O'Neil sons Jerry is the one who, perhaps, looks most like both his mother and father. He has his father's blue eyes and some other W.O. physical characteristics, but he resembles his mother, too. And another thing Jerry inherited from W.O. is a complete disregard for time so far as business is concerned.

He travels a great deal, mostly by company plane. He visits the tire plants at Mayfield, Kentucky, and Waco, Texas, as well as the synthetic complex at Odessa, Texas, when an important decision is to be made. The same is true of trips to the chemical plants and the plastics operations at Jeannette, Pennsylvania; Lawrence, Massachusetts; and Toledo, Ohio. There have been times when he was on a virtual commuting schedule between Akron and Aerojet-General in California.

Jerry's annual flight mileage has never been officially logged, but he must be one of the five or six highest-mileage top executives in the United States. There are two reasons for his constant travel: first, the number of General plants throughout the country, and, second, the fact that Jerry likes to make decisions on the spot, face to face with the people who have the problem or the responsibility for carrying out procedures. He dislikes to handle important matters by correspondence. Any letter he writes he tries to confine to one page. And those in the company who write to him seem to feel that theirs get a better reaction if also held to a single page.

Jerry conducts a good deal of his business by long-distance telephone, but he is not the compulsive user of the telephone that Tom and John are. The three talk to one another by phone frequently.

Since Jerry's election to the presidency the company has had a most impressive growth record. Sales for the five years from 1960 to 1964 more than doubled those of the preceding five years. They amounted to about $4.7 billion compared to $2.25 billion. In 1963, sales exceeded a billion dollars for the first time in company history, and repeated in 1964. Profits, after taxes, set a new company high in 1963, or $34.6 million, to be exceeded in 1964 by a profit of $36.9 million. For the five-year period, from 1960 through 1964, net profits were considerably more than $125 million.

The common-stock equity per share rose from $8.48 in 1960 to $14.72 in 1964. Another most impressive statistic is that earned surplus rose from $81.9 million in 1960 to more than $180 million in 1964.

In 1964 RKO General and Aerojet-General, which for a number of years had retained their entire earnings, resumed the payment of dividends. In 1964, too, the dividend on General Tire common stock was increased to sixty cents a share. This makes General's dividend commitment about $9 million a year on both its common and preferred stock.

While General's dividend requirements are amply met by its current earnings, Jerry points out that they are fortified by the earning potential of RKO General and Aerojet-General, both of which are highly profitable and have expanding potentials in the new areas they have developed.

A big factor in the increase in General's business in tires during Jerry's administration has been the addition of the production of the Mayfield, Kentucky, plant. Construction of this facility—General's third domestic plant—was started in 1959 and, from the drawing-board stage, was one of Jerry's special responsibilities as W.O.'s Executive Assistant. The Mayfield plant is probably the most modern and efficient tire plant in the United States. Having it has enabled General to increase its sales of original-equipment tires to automobile manufacturers greatly and has made it possible for the company to take on a number of important special-brands accounts.

A single visual symbol to identify all the many products and services of The General Tire & Rubber Company was adopted under Jerry's administration. Basic to the program was the alignment of all the company's activities under six divisions. Then the new *Big G* trademark, in bold, distinctive type, was created as the over-all umbrella. The Big G symbol remains instantly recognizable as the company's image-maker-in-type for all the divisions including General Tires for all kinds of vehicles; RKO General; Aerojet-General; the Chemical/Plastics Division; and the Industrial Products Division. Type changes within the bold Big G, or directly under it, enable the basic identifying symbol to be adapted specifically to each Division and to remain instantly recognizable to the public.

The adoption of the Big G trademark has relieved a nagging backache which afflicts all modern companies which are widely diversified. It solved the problem of providing quick identification of the parent company and permitted specific application to each of its subsidiaries and products. Few companies are more widely diversified than General Tire, and still fewer have solved their identification problem—a first step in creating a widely known public image—as neatly as General's Big G device.

The principal products and services of the six divisions are summarized in the Appendix, with the names of their officers in General's Fiftieth Year.

Afterword

Since W.O. considered Introductions, Forewords, and Appendixes a nuisance, this "Afterword"—written during General's Fiftieth Year—might be the proper place to reflect upon Bill O'Neil the man. General Tire, inextricably woven into the threads of American business life, is unlike so many other companies. It bears the indelible stamp of one family.

Perhaps the distinguishing feature of the O'Neils' stewardship is the ability of all its members to anticipate new trends and thus guide General through its years of social and industrial expansion. This inheritance, bridging fifty years, stems from Michael, one of the first entrepreneurs to turn from the limited and local dry-goods store to the increasing services of a department store. Michael's vision took root in Will, whose foresight in establishing a replacement-tire market through a system of exclusive dealers set the pattern for Tom's work in commercial and pay-television, Jerry's emphasis upon new methods of management and insight into the fields of chemistry and plastics. John's handling of financial architecture and company pensions, charitable funds, and profit-sharing programs has been a model for many corporations. Even the son who spent only a very brief time with General—Bill, Jr.—left his imprint on the company; it was his personal success in radio that led the company into that field and, indirectly and by coincidence, into Aerojet.

As always, W.O. generated the dynamism responsible for the ambition of his sons. The ever-increasing tempo of his life, the continual concern for people, and the expansion of his responsibilities were the hallmarks that dictated his life. He admired energy and decisiveness even in a competitor and often turned another's success to his advantage.

One example of this was W.O.'s full-page advertisement applauding Goodyear's sponsorship of a weekly radio program dramatizing Fulton Oursler's best-selling book on the life of Christ, *The Greatest Story Ever Told*. Concerned with an apparent shift in moral values stemming from the chaos of the Second World War, W.O. felt that the Goodyear program was performing a valuable public service and that it should be given proper recognition.

Under the headline, "We suggest you listen to 'The Greatest Story Ever Told,'" the text read:

This is an unusual advertisement. It invites you to listen to a radio program of a competitor of ours.

This program is broadcast every Sunday at 6:30 P.M. (Eastern Standard Time) over the nationwide facilities of the American Broadcasting Company. It is called "The Greatest Story Ever Told" and is sponsored by The Goodyear Tire and Rubber Company.

Perhaps you have heard it. It draws upon incidents in the Bible to refresh people's minds about the most radical doctrine ever preached.

It could not be broadcast in Russia.

It would disturb the Russian worker to know that man is not the tool of the state—to be enslaved and denied the fruits of his labor; to be disenfranchised, displaced, interned or liquidated by political whim. It would disillusion him to know that there is a government under which, by simply having faith in God and a decent respect for one another's rights, as members of His family, he can live more happily than by giving in to despair of Him and hate for one another.

"The Greatest Story Ever Told" has all the impact of news —radical news for a world beset by the suspicion and hate which Communism spreads and feeds on.

It reminds us that without faith men have no moral yardstick by which to judge the motives of their leaders.

This we have seen happen in the totalitarian states of our own times—ever since World War I, when the unmoral leaders of materialistic Germany used Lenin to spread the cancer of atheistic Communism through Russia as a germ weapon of that war. This same insidious weapon is being beamed toward us.

At the core of this evil is an unmoral Godless ambition which is the competitor of the American social ideal—as the criminal, without morals, is the competitor of the honest man.

This is the iron rule of Communism which a handful of vengeful people would substitute for the Golden Rule among us.

The merchandisers of discontent have been selling a dishonest product for too long a time.

Listening to a radio program may seem a small weapon against so grave a danger. But unless the great majority of us deem it worthwhile to renew our faith in the Source of our power and blessings, we may not find the strength to preserve them.

The advertisement was not personally signed by William O'Neil, but simply by The General Tire & Rubber

Company, Akron, Ohio. It appeared in Sunday editions of *The New York Times,* New York *Herald Tribune,* Washington *Star,* Washington *Times Herald,* Chicago *Tribune,* Detroit *News,* Detroit *Free Press,* Boston *Globe,* Boston *Herald,* Indianapolis *Star,* Waco *Tribune Herald,* San Francisco *Chronicle,* Miami *Herald,* Cleveland *Plain Dealer,* Akron *Beacon Journal,* Philadelphia *Bulletin,* and St. Louis *Globe-Democrat.*

Charles F. Burke, the very efficient assistant to W.O. for so many years, reported that more than a thousand letters and telegrams of congratulation poured in. The public response, spontaneous and congratulatory, evoked editorials in many major American newspapers.

In W.O.'s time, General Tire was reputed to be the largest business in the country without an organization chart. The reason for this was W.O.'s often-expressed opinion that "a system is a poor substitute for brains."

When the business was pretty much confined to tires that "cost more because they are worth more," W.O. had an occult method of handpicking individuals for assignments that went on for years and bore no relation to their primary jobs. An example of this was J. E. Anderson, an auditor, whose office was tucked away in a remote corner and could be found only by the most knowledgeable in the organization, who bought all the automobiles for General, its test fleets, and salesmen's cars from coast to coast. W.O.'s instinct about people made the standard corporate chart all but impossible.

Actually, there is still no great emphasis on a formal organization chart. But despite the company's complexity, its organization is streamlined. Any top executive can chart on the back of an envelope the lines of authority. There is, however, within the company's various divisions a tremendous pool of scientific, engineering, financial, legal, marketing, and production experience. Very often the specialized capabilities of an individual in one division will be lent to help solve the problems of another. This is in the tradition of what Gil Swart of Akron research did in the early days of General's association with Aerojet to confirm the link which W.O. suspected existed between rubber and rocket-propellant chemistry. And Dr. A. L. Antonio of Aerojet returned the favor a few years later by helping to establish the uniform quality of the PVC resins at the new Ashtabula plant. The difference is that today these assignments are for the duration of the problem only. In the old days, they were permanent and carried on as an interesting sideline, a relief from the monotony of one job.

Practically all of General's ventures into new product fields have been successful, but two were not. Both deserve to be recalled because they appeared at crucial periods and were highly creative answers to problems of their times. They were discontinued when the conditions which created the need for them changed.

The first was the Frostair, a large-capacity deep-freeze and regular electrical refrigerator in one unit for the home. W.O. became interested in it shortly before World War II began. He was concerned about what tire rationing would do to the business of General's dealers and believed that food conservation would be an important fact of life. The Frostair was built by one of the leading names in commercial refrigeration and W.O. was assured that the government would give a high priority to the motors and compressors needed. Unfortunately, under wartime conditions, motors and compressors became almost as difficult to get as rationed tires. When they did become obtainable again, after the war, W.O.'s old conviction that General Tire dealers should stay out of the hardware business reasserted itself. The remaining inventory of Frostairs—the first single-unit deep-freeze and regular refrigerator, and the first with the "frost-free" feature—was sold to an exporter to South American countries.

W.O.'s only remembered remark of regret about the Frostair was "I'm the only fellow who ever got burned on a refrigerator."

The other item, born of necessity and consigned to limbo by the birth of the space age, was a plumbing fixture. Because Aerojet-General has become the nation's largest organization devoted to the development and manufacture of rocket motors and propellants, the fact that the company was trying to establish itself in the "swing-spout" business immediately after the war will come as a surprise to most people.

This device was a kitchen-sink spout which could be swung out of the way. Surveys proved that the new construction and replacement markets for it were tremendous. Manufacture was begun, but this was one time that General found itself completely out of its element. The "swing spout" went down the drain with the dawn of the space age, and Aerojet-General was first on the launching pad.

W.O. always referred to himself as "a tire manufacturer." Tires continued to be his chief interest all his life. His roots were in Akron, and he had a lifelong attachment to rubber—and tires. His instinctive feeling that he was "a tire man" never really changed. All the news headlines given to General's spectacular growth in radio and TV, for instance, he seemed to value most as "good publicity for General Tires." However, he chose all of General's fields of diversification and took an active interest in them.

Jerry, because he worked with the department heads and personnel at the home office in Akron for more than ten years before his father's death, has the same kind of close, informal rapport with them that W.O. had with his smaller organization. He likes to have small meetings in his office on problems as they arise with the people involved. His desire to give the company's various divisions autonomy, to work out their own problems under the umbrella of General Tire policy, is pointed up by the fact that each Division now is organized under its own head who has the title of President.

Jerry shares W.O.'s restless enthusiasm for new ideas. He realizes, however, in this day of more advanced technologies, that the utmost in scientific research is required to develop new products and new processes.

"Dad's faith in the power of new ideas is the reason why he started General Tire in the first place," Jerry points out. "At first, the ideas were relatively simple, commonsense improvements on pretty primitive tires. But before World War II, Dad saw that the technologies were moving ahead faster than the nonscientific approach could cope with. That's why General assumed early leadership in research and development, all out of proportion to the relatively small size of the company then. This set the pattern for our great postwar expansion of our research-and-development facilities. And this foresight was the key to much of our growth—probably most of it. I think the greatest legacy Dad left the company was his faith in ideas and his early commitment to scientific research and development."

It is a curious fact that Tom, interviewed in New York without previous knowledge of what Jerry had said, also emphasized W.O.'s dedication to the world of new ideas. But from a little different viewpoint.

He said:

"I never heard Dad say, 'Things are going along all right, let's not rock the boat.' In fact, when things were going too smoothly, he seemed to become suspicious that the company was in danger of becoming complacent. He had a dozen new ideas himself every day, and he would listen to anyone who had one. I think it may have been his early exposure to Aerojet and the fantastic scientific breakthroughs they were developing that awakened his first interest in the modern scientific investigation of ideas. At any rate, at about that time he began to put a lot of money into scientific research and development, which has kept us ahead of competition and provided the thrust into profitable new industries."

"He was always looking for something new" is the way John O'Neil summarizes one of his father's most prominent characteristics, which is basically the point Jerry and Tom made, except that John's remarks took on more of a financial tone—which is understandable—as his remarks continued:

"I think Dad was the best window-shopper I ever saw. He would listen to any idea, any business proposition, large or small. It's because of this we own RKO, Aerojet and, less directly, why we are in the chemical-plastics business. Even our international operations started with Dad's listening to the problems of the men from Mexico City."

Then John added: "Dad often used to quote a business associate of his who said, 'Business is just practice.' Dad always kept himself in practice and even at the age of seventy-five was still looking for new business worlds to conquer."

All three sons of W.O. in the business are extremely conscious of the imprint left by their father on practically every phase of the company. And their loyalty to his memory manifests itself best when, in reminiscing about him, they clearly acknowledge feeling an urgent obligation to move General Tire along, as far and as fast in their day as he did in his.

They feel that in each division of the company there is "a whale of a territory" to develop. All their products and services are faced to the future. And so are they.

In early 1966 there were thirty-two grandchildren of Will and Grace O'Neil. All are living except Hugh, Jr., the Carnegie Medalist.

William is married to Miriam Loretta Cotter, and they have two sons, William III and Brian.

Thomas is married to Claire McCahey, and they have a family of nine—Shane, Eileen, Mark, Conn Michael, Claire, Liam, Grace, Carol, and Owen. Thus, Thomas' grandfather is represented by Conn Michael; his father by Liam, the Gaelic form of William, and his mother by Grace.

John is married to Helene Connellan, and they have four children, Helene, John James, Jr., Ann, and Jane.

Hugh O'Neil, who was married to Jean Palmer, has a surviving son, Rory.

Michael G. (Jerry) O'Neil, is married to Juliet Rudolph, and they have seven children: Michael G., Jr., Gregory John, Jeffrey Sean, Shawn, Julie, Nancy, and Susan.

The only daughter of Bill and Grace O'Neil, Grace, is married to William Regan, and they have eight children: Grace Mary, William Mahon, Jr., John O'Neil, Hugh, Neil, Jane, and Mary and Ann, who are twins.

Appendix

Aㅤsummary of General Tire's divisions, subsidiaries, affiliates, top personnel, products, and services was compiled during General's Fiftieth Anniversary Year by Edward B. Butler, Director of Public Relations. The summary is remarkably concise considering the complexity of General's modern operations in the many fields into which it was first led by W.O.'s restless, imaginative enterprise. It is appended here as a panoramic view of the company and its activities in 1965.

Headquarters (Domestic and Foreign Operations): Akron, Ohio. Tire Facilities: Akron, Ohio; Waco, Texas; Mayfield, Kentucky. Produce all types of tires and tubes. Also located in Akron: Central Engineering, Tire Development, Research and Development Center. Sales offices for Tire, Chemical/Plastics, Athletic Goods, and the General Tire International Company.

One of the nation's leading producers of tires and tubes, General manufactures more than 1800 types and sizes for every conceivable purpose—for trucks, automobiles, earth-moving equipment, farm machinery, small trailers, and aircraft.

Chemical/Plastics Division, Headquarters: Akron, Ohio. The Chemical and Plastics operations of The General Tire & Rubber Company are consolidated into one division, the Chemical/Plastics Division.

General Tire has chemical-manufacturing plants at Ashtabula, Ohio; Mogadore, Ohio; and Odessa, Texas; with division and sales offices located at the Akron headquarters of the company. Chemical products include Synthetic Rubber (SBR), Polyvinyl Chloride, Resin, Latices used in the textile, paint, rubber, and paper industries and other specialty chemicals.

Also, General Tire has a substantial interest in Phillips Chemical Company's polybutadiene rubber operations near Borger, Texas.

It has plastic plants at Toledo, Ohio; Lawrence, Massachusetts; Jeannette, Pennsylvania; and Columbus, Mississippi. It has a reinforced plastics facility at Marion, Indiana. Polyfoam-manufacturing facilities are at Marion, Indiana, and City of Orange, California. Polyfoam fabricating plants are located in Tampa, Florida; Atlanta, Georgia; and Birmingham, Alabama. Sales and engineering services are generally directed from the respective plants, with over-all policy originating from Akron.

Bolta Products Division, Lawrence, Massachusetts. New York Office: 349 Fifth Avenue. Vinyl materials for home, office, and automobile; vinyl counter and table-top material; expanded vinyls for upholstery, outerwear, and novelty uses; rigid plastics products for a variety of industrial uses.

Pennsylvania Division, National Sales Offices, Pennsylvania Athletic Goods, Pennsylvania Sponge Rubber, Akron, Ohio. Facilities: Jeannette, Pennsylvania.

Textileather Division, Toledo, Ohio. Vinyl materials for automotive and furniture upholstery, luggage and leather goods; motion-picture screens and window shades; sporting goods; bookbinding; aircraft interiors and upholstery; footwear, protective clothing, garments; custom industrial products, synthetic textiles.

Columbus Plastics Facility, Columbus, Mississippi. Calendered, printed, and embossed supported and unsupported vinyl sheeting for home furnishings, marine, shoe, and automotive industries.

Marion Facility, Marion, Indiana. Polyfoam for furniture, automotive, and aircraft cushioning, insulation applications, mattresses, automotive toppers; custom molded, flexible, and rigid Polyfoam for automotive, bus, aircraft, and furniture applications; fiberglass-reinforced polyester laminates designed and produced to customer requirements for automotive, aircraft, appliance, electrical, recreation, military, and communication industries, molded premix and resin-impregnated wood-fiber shapes with decorative and custom-painted surfaces.

General Metal Products, Cuyahoga Falls, Ohio. Aircraft wheels and brakes, industrial wheels and hubs; special rubber machinery; tools and dies; molds for rubber and plastics materials.

Industrial Products Division, Headquarters: Wabash, Indiana. Facilities: Wabash, Evansville, and Logansport, Indiana. Industrial products designed and produced to customer specifications; extruded flexible and rigid plastics; magnetic tapes; metal stampings; Silentbloc vibration mountings; glass-run channel automotive components; gas masks; molded missile liners; a variety of other products and components for the aircraft, automotive, appliance, electrical, recreation, and communication industries and the military.

In 1965 the Industrial Products Division's Welland, Ontario (Canada) facility was merged with Mansfield Rubber (Canada) Ltd. into a new Canadian organization, Mansfield-Denman General, Ltd. Tire-manufacturing facility located at Barrie, Ontario.

Aerojet-General Corporation, once known solely as a developer of rocket propulsion, is now a diversified technical company with an extremely wide range of scientific, engineering, and manufacturing capabilities. Aerojet remains the nation's number-one producer of rocket power for aerospace applications (solid fuel, liquid fuel, and nuclear), but activities also cover a broad field including electronics, architecture, instrumentation, optics, biological detection systems, infrared sensing devices, automation, advanced structural materials, oceanography, life sciences, nucleonics, torpedoes, ordnance, chemistry, heavy and light manufacturing.

Aerojet facilities are located in Azusa, El Monte, Sacramento, Covina, Chino, Downey, Riverside, and San Ramon, California; Homestead, Florida; Batesville, Arkansas; Frederick, Maryland; and Plainview, New York.

The corporate structure of *RKO General, Inc.* includes TV stations in such important markets as New York, Los Angeles, Boston, Memphis, and Windsor–Detroit; radio stations in the same markets, plus San Francisco and Washington, D.C.; the Yankee Network in New England; RKO General Phonevision in Hartford, Connecticut, for its Subscription TV experiment; RKO Sound Studios in New York City; and Eastern Broadcasting Company in Boston. In 1961, RKO General acquired Vumore, Inc., Oklahoma City, owner and operator of community antenna systems, and Video Independent Theatres, Inc., also headquartered in Oklahoma City, operator of 126 motion picture theaters in Oklahoma, Texas, New Mexico, Mississippi, and Kansas. RKO General, Inc., also owns the Pittsburgh Outdoor Advertising Company, Pittsburgh, Pennsylvania; Electronics Leasing Corporation, New York; The Equinox House, Inc. (a summer-resort hotel located in Manchester, Vermont). It has controlling interest in Frontier Airlines, Inc. (a regional airline based in Denver, Colorado).

In 1964 and early 1965, RKO General, Inc. acquired 48 per cent interest in the Schenectady (New York) *Union-Star* and has a ten-year option to purchase the remaining interest in the newspaper; 56.6 per cent of the stock of Fleetwood Corporation, a Canadian manufacturer of home electronics equipment, television sets, radios, hi-fi, stereo, and phonographs; and 65.9 per cent of Citadel Industries, Inc.

A. M. Byers Company, Pittsburgh, Pennsylvania. Wrought-iron pipe and flat-rolled products; merchant steel pipe. Galis Manufacturing Company is a subsidiary of A. M. Byers. It has five plants, in Fairmont, West Virginia (2); Morgantown, West Virginia; Bluefield, West Virginia; and Ernest, Pennsylvania. The Galis companies manufacture and repair electrical motors, material-handling equipment, and underground mining equipment for the coal- and metal-mining as well as nonmetallic mining industries.

In 1965, the Missouri Steel Castings and Missouri-Rogers Corporation were acquired. They were merged into a subsidiary, The Missouri-Rogers Corporation, operating in manufacture of equipment serving the coal mining, crushed stone, gravel, and other industries.

General Tire's operations outside the U.S. include:
Argentina, Buenos Aires: Neumaticos General Argentina, S.A. Tires, tubes, and repair materials.

[237]

Canada, Toronto, Ontario: The General Tire & Rubber Company of Canada, Ltd. Tires, tubes, accessories, and repair materials.

Chile, Santiago: Industria Nacional de Neumaticos, S.A. Tires, tubes, batteries, belting, and flooring.

Ecuador, Cuenca: Ecuadorian Rubber Company, C.A. Tires, tubes, accessories, and repair materials.

Holland, Amsterdam: The General Tire & Rubber Company—Holland N.V. Tires, tubes, and repair materials.

Iran, Teheran: The General Tire & Rubber Company of Iran. Tubes, tires, repair materials.

Mexico, Mexico City: General Popo, S.A. Tires, tubes, batteries, and miscellaneous rubber products.

Morocco, Casablanca: The General Tire & Rubber Company of Morocco. Tires, tubes, and repair materials.

Pakistan, Landhi: The General Tyre & Rubber Company of Pakistan. Tires, tubes, and repair materials.

Portugal, Lousada: Manufactura Nacional de Borracha, S.A.R.L. Tires, tubes, and repair materials.

Portugal, Lousada: Industria Textil do Ave., S.A.R.L. Textile and cord fabric.

South Africa, Port Elizabeth: The General Tire & Rubber Company (South Africa) Ltd. Tires, tubes, accessories, and repair materials.

Spain, Torrelavega: General Fábrica Española del Caucho, S.A. Tires, tubes, camelback, repair materials, molded and mechanical rubber goods.

Venezuela, Caracas: Compania Anonima Nacional Manufacturera de Caucho y Neumaticos *GENERAL*. Tires, tubes, and miscellaneous rubber products.

Venezuela, Valencia: Fábrica Nacional de Recuperacion, C.A. Manufacture of reclaim rubber.

Venezuela, Valencia: C. A. de Productos Nacionales *GENERAL*. Rubber goods, plastics, flooring, and tiling.

Affiliates:

Argentina, Buenos Aires: FATE, S.A. Ind. Com. E Inmob.

Germany, Munich: Metzeler Gummiwerke, A.G.

Guatemala, Guatemala City: General Tire and Incatecu, S.A. "Ginsa."

Italy, Turin: CEAT Gomma.

Japan, Osaka: The Toyo Rubber Industry Company, Ltd.

Aerojet subsidiaries outside the U.S.:

England, Banwell: Weston-Super-Mare, Bristol Aerojet Limited (affiliation with Bristol Aeroplane Company Limited). Rocket and missile metal parts.

France, Neuilly-sur-Seine: Aerojet-General International Corporation (subsidiary of Aerojet-General Corporation).

Germany, Bonn: Orion-Aerojet GmbH. Proposed rocket applications.

In addition to these corporate divisions, subsidiaries, and affiliates, General administers its own pension funds. It is one of fewer than 1 per cent of American industries to do so. The plan, put into effect in 1947 by John O'Neil and still administered by him, has grown from an original investment of $1,050,000 to a total corpus which reached $165 million in 1965. Approximately 50,000 employees of General Tire, Aerojet-General, RKO General, and A. M. Byers are covered. Profit-sharing funds and charitable foundations have been added. The funds provide a high degree of security and benefits have been increased three times.

The Board of Directors of The General Tire & Rubber Company is composed of fourteen members.

Members of the Board, the date of their appointment to the Board, and their present business connections follow:

T. F. O'Neil, Director since December 12, 1948, was elected Chairman of the Board April 4, 1961; Chairman of the Board, RKO General, Inc., subsidiary of General Tire.

M. G. O'Neil, Director since April 4, 1950, was elected President of The General Tire & Rubber Company April 5, 1960.

John O'Neil, reappointed Director April 5, 1955, is Chairman Finance Committee. He served as Treasurer and Director in the late 1940s but had resigned early in 1950.

L. A. McQueen, Director since April 3, 1945, Honorary Chairman of the Board and Chairman of the Executive Committee.

Dan A. Kimball, reappointed Director January 21, 1953, after leave of absence to serve as Secretary of the Navy. Originally appointed to the Board December 28, 1948. He is Vice-President, Aerojet Operations; Chairman of the Executive Committee of the Aerojet-General Corporation, subsidiary of The General Tire & Rubber Company.

Robert Iredell, Director since February 4, 1941; retired

[241]

September 1, 1952, as Director of Engineering, The General Tire & Rubber Co.

C. F. O'Neil, Director since April 4, 1944. Vice-President in charge of Foreign Operations from April 2, 1946, until his retirement on June 30, 1963. [Died July 1965]

Charles J. Jahant, Director since December 27, 1928. Vice-President in charge of Manufacturing from December 23, 1934, until his retirement on April 7, 1964.

Edmund W. Ross, Director since April 4, 1950; President and Director, The C.P.A. Insurance Company, Detroit, Michigan.

Frank W. Knowlton, Director since January 26, 1952; Vice-President and General Counsel, The General Tire & Rubber Company. A member of General's legal staff since 1929.

Samuel S. Poor, Director since April 3, 1945, is retired. He served as Vice-President in Charge of Merchandising, The General Tire & Rubber Company, from February 6, 1940, to July 25, 1951.

O. G. Vinnedge, Director since April 1, 1958. A rubber executive for thirty-four years, he is Vice-President in charge of the Industrial Products Division, The General Tire & Rubber Company.

John E. Powers, Director since January 7, 1959, is Vice President–Marketing, The General Tire & Rubber Company.

William E. Zisch, Director since April 2, 1963, is President of Aerojet-General Corporation, subsidiary of The General Tire & Rubber Company.

Principal officers of The General Tire & Rubber Company:

T. F. O'Neil, Chairman of the Board of Directors
M. G. O'Neil, President
John O'Neil, Chairman Finance Committee
L. A. McQueen, Chairman, Executive Committee
Dan A. Kimball, Vice-President in charge of Aerojet Operations
John E. Powers, Vice-President–Marketing
F. W. Knowlton, Vice-President; General Counsel
Wendell J. Gurtner, Treasurer
Tress E. Pittenger, Secretary

Principal operating officers of divisions and subsidiaries:

Sam Salem, President, Chemical/Plastics division
Morgan J. Morgan, President, Tire division
John B. Poor, President, RKO General, Inc.
W. E. Zisch, President, Aerojet-General Corporation
F. A. Duffy, President, General Tire International
James L. Wetzel, President, A. M. Byers Company
O. G. Vinnedge, President, Industrial Products division
J. J. Mulcahy, Vice-President–Manufacturers' Sales

[243]

Other corporate officers:

E. W. Lutz, Assistant Treasurer *

J. L. Wade, Assistant Secretary

John J. Dalton, Assistant Secretary

William R. Ealy, Assistant Treasurer

Other division and subsidiary officers:

RKO GENERAL BROADCASTING

Hathaway Watson, President

CHEMICAL/PLASTICS DIVISION

George Hackim, Vice-President–Industrial Sales

H. J. Peppercorn, Vice-President–Manufacturing

J. H. Miller, Vice-President–Controller

J. A. Kleinhans, Vice-President–Chemical Operations

TIRE DIVISION

J. S. Hanse, Vice-President

J. W. Frasche, Vice-President, Manufacturing

P. E. Shobert, Vice-President–Original Equipment Operations

INDUSTRIAL PRODUCTS DIVISION

H. M. Garver, Vice-President–Operations

H. C. Sommer, Vice-President–Industrial Sales

AEROJET-GENERAL

L. Wayne Mullane, Group Vice-President

A. L. Antonio, Group Vice-President

W. L. Gore, Senior Vice-President–Sales

K. F. Mundt, Senior Vice-President

R. I. McKenzie, Vice-President, Treasurer

T. Edward Beehan, Secretary **

* *Retired December 1, 1965.*
** *Retired February 2, 1966.*

[244]

INDEX

[249]

ABOUT THE AUTHOR

Dennis John O'Neill (not a member of the Akron O'Neil clan) is a native of Indiana. On graduation from Notre Dame in 1926, he became a special editorial assistant to Boyd Gurley, editor of the Indianapolis *Times,* a Scripps-Howard paper crusading against the Ku Klux Klan, then rampant in Indiana and dominant in state politics. O'Neill worked with Gurley in the exposé that broke the Klan's power in Indiana and for which the *Times* was awarded the Pulitzer Prize in 1928. O'Neill then moved to Scripps-Howard's news-feature arm, Newspaper Enterprise Association; his daily column "American Almanac" was used by more than 700 dailies. He was also Associate Editor of the Sunday-newspaper magazine *Every Week.*

O'Neill left journalism for advertising and for many years was an executive of the D'Arcy Advertising Company in Cleveland, from which he resigned in 1962 to travel and write. As Vice-President and creative head of D'Arcy in Cleveland he had a close rapport with Bill O'Neil; during an association of more than twenty years he gained an intimate knowledge of W.O.'s business philosophy as well as a respect and admiration for the man.

Dennis O'Neill is the publisher of *The Ancestral Map of Ireland,* a work that began as a hobby, depicts the patrimony, origin, lineage, and social status of a thousand pre-seventeenth-century Irish families, and is regarded as the standard work in its field.

Mr. and Mrs. O'Neill have six children and fourteen grandchildren.

Frontispiece: portrait of W. O'Neil by DAVID PHILIP WILSON.

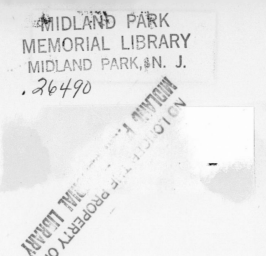